HANNIE RAYSON co-founded Theatreworks in 1981 following six years of tertiary study from which she gained a Bachelor of Arts from Melbourne University and a Diploma of Arts in Dramatic Arts from The Victorian College of Arts.

Since 1984 she has worked as Writer-In-Residence with several companies including The Mill Theatre, Latrobe and Monash Universities and Playbox. She has received a Fellowship from the Literature Board of the Australia Council.

She is the author of *Please Return to Sender, Leave it Til Monday, Mary, Room to Move*, and a teleplay, *Sloth*, which is part of the ABC series, *The Seven Deadly Sins*.

In 1985 *Room to Move* was premiered by Playbox with Theatreworks. It was subsequently produced throughout Australia and won the 1986 Australian Writers' Guild Award for Best Original Stage Play.

Hotel Sorrento was commissioned by Playbox for the premiere season at the C.U.B. Malthouse, Melbourne in 1991. The production, directed by Aubrey Mellor, was presented by the Sydney Theatre Company in 1991, and other productions followed in Perth, Canberra and Brisbane.

For *Hotel Sorrento*, Hannie won the Australian Writers' Guild Award for Best New Play, the New South Wales Literary Award for Best New Play and the Victorian Green Room Award.

W9-BDW-795

For Kathy and Suzie Skelton

PHOTO ACKNOWLEDGEMENTS: p.3 Above: Peter Curtin as Dick and Julia Blake as Marge in the Playbox production of *Hotel Sorrento*, 1990. Photographer: Jeff Busby. Below: Elspeth Ballantyne as Hilary and Robin Cuming as Wal in the Sydney Theatre Company production. Photographer: Branco Gaica. p.23 Above: Peter Curtin as Dick and Jennifer Claire as Marge in the STC production. Below: Caroline Gillmer as Meg and David Latham as Edwin in the Playbox production. p.47 Above Elspeth Ballantyne as Hilary and Genevieve Picot as Pippa in the Playbox production. Below: David Latham as Edwin and Peter Curtin as Dick in the same production. p.83 Barry Otto as Edwin and Jennifer Claire as Marge in the STC production.

FILM STILLS
p.89 John Hargreaves as Dick and Joan Plowright as Marge. p.90 Above: Nicholas Bell as Edwin and Caroline Goodall as Meg. Below: Ben Thomas as Troy and Tara Morice as Pippa. p.95 Above: Tara Morice as Pippa, Caroline Goodall as Meg and Caroline Gillmer as Hilary. Below: Nicholas Bell as Edwin and John Hargreaves as Dick. From the 1995 Bayside Pictures film *Hotel Sorrento*. Stills Photography: Suzie Woods. Reproduced by courtesy of Beyond Films Limited.

HOTEL
SORRENTO

HANNIE RAYSON

CURRENCY PRESS • SYDNEY

CURRENCY PLAYS
General Editor: Katharine Brisbane

First published 1990 by Currency Press Pty Ltd
Revised edition published 1992
This further revised edition published 1995
Reprinted 1996, 1997, 1998
by Currency Press Ltd
PO Box 2287, Strawberry Hills,
NSW 2012 Australia
www.currency.com.au

Copyright © Hannie Rayson, 1992 *Hotel Sorrento*

This book is copyright. Apart from any fair dealing for the purpose of private study, research or review, as permitted under the Copyright Act, no part may be reproduced by any process without written permission. Inquiries concerning publication, translation or recording rights should be addressed to the publishers.

Any performance or public reading of *Hotel Sorrento* is forbidden unless a licence has been received from the author or the author's agent. The purchase of this book in no way gives the purchaser the right to perform the play in public, whether by means of a staged production or a reading. All applications for public performance should be made to the author, c/o Hilary Linstead and Associates, Level 8, Plaza 11, 500 Oxford Street, Bondi Jcn, NSW 2022, Australia

NATIONAL LIBRARY OF AUSTRALIA CIP DATA
Rayson, Hannie, 1957-
    Hotel Sorrento.
    ISBN 0 86819 337 2
    I. Title.
A822.3

Printed by Australian Print Group, Maryborough, VIC
Cover design by Anaconda Graphic Design/Trevor Hood
Cover photo shows John Hargreaves as Dick and Joan Plowright as Marge in the 1995 Bayside Pictures film *Hotel Sorrento*.

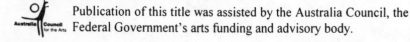 Publication of this title was assisted by the Australia Council, the Federal Government's arts funding and advisory body.

CONTENTS

A Sweet Pensive Sadness

Hannie Rayson

With *Hotel Sorrento* I wanted to write a play of ideas; something which would send an audience out into the night with all sorts of things to talk about over coffee. I also wanted to create a 'sweet pensive sadness' to pervade the experience, as there is something delectable about melancholy which seems to alter the way we see things.

To date my plays have been a response to particular contemporary social phenomena which I want to understand more fully. I am interested in subject matter which is bursting with contradiction. As a playwright I am concerned with the task of posing questions, both in the process of writing and in the finished work. As a dramatic device it allows me to activate and engage an audience but perhaps more importantly it is a vehicle for both playwright and audience to embark upon a genuine line of enquiry together.

With *Hotel Sorrento* my central question was how far we had come in terms of our quest to articulate an Australian identity and what kinds of changes had taken place during the past decade. I was interested in how the experience of living elsewhere alters one's perceptions of home. And, conversely, for those who've stayed and contributed to the life of the culture from 'the inside', where is the line between a healthy nationalism and blind patriotism?

I decided to focus on the relationship between literature and cultural identity and to exploit the debate in critical/literary circles about Australian fiction. To merely hold a mirror to reflect ourselves and our culture does not automatically constitute great art, some argued. In our bid to be counted as a country with important cultural heroes and myths were we overstating the calibre of our cultural products? Could we really look for profundity and passion in our own literature?

My interest also was to try and weave themes of cultural identity through several layers of the narrative, so I could explore ideas about loyalty, for example, or betrayal, from the perspective of the expatriate's response to her country, her fiction and her family.

In 1986 I went to London on a research grant from the then Theatre Board of the Australia Council to do a series of interviews with expatriates. Peter Carey's face was in all the bookshop windows and on sandwich boards on the street. He had been nominated for The Booker prize for his novel *Illywhacker*, and whilst he didn't win that year, Oz literature was a talking point.

In an interview in *The Times*, Carey said that he had lived in London for two years from 1968 and loved it like any other visitor. 'But one day I looked at the man at the local service station and suddenly realised that if I lived here ten years I wouldn't know that man any better. I decided to go home . . . What I missed was that ability to recognise instantly what people are, what they are thinking and feeling which comes effortlessly with your own kind.'

At this point, the idea of a novelist as my central character was born and that of her Booker-nominated novel forming the backbone of the play. I needed to create someone whose opinions were going to receive attention by the world press; someone passionate and outspoken about Australia so that the pendulum between my own sense of deep affection and frustration that this country can engender, could swing back and forth freely. In this way I could create a tension and interplay of often contradictory ideas. But at the heart of this play is the family and the sisters.

'Few other relationships can inspire such loyalty or such anger as sisters. Sisters can experience great closeness, but when they fall out, the conflicts go deeper too.' *Sisters on Sisters*, Jane Dowdeswell, Grapevine, U.K. 1988.

Although I have no sisters, I used to think that the long term bonds I've made with certain women friends were of the same ilk. But in writing this play and observing sisters over a long period, it is clear that sisters have something else. One thing that interests me is the volatility that is often a feature of the relationship: knowing intuitively and often unwittingly how to ignite a fuse and start a spot fire, which may rage out of control or be extinguished quickly. And yet despite this, families seem to have an astonishing capacity to endlessly postpone the settling of conflicts and old scores.

In the writing and subsequent production of this play, Playbox have been stalwart supporters. I am indebted to them for their encouragement and patience and to The Performing Arts Board and Literature Boards of the Australia Council, for their support.

I especially want to acknowledge the contribution of my friend and dramaturg Hilary Glow. With talk into the wee small hours, the patient reading of draft upon draft, and the constant challenge of her intellect, she has been a sustaining and inspiring force.

I also wish to express my gratitude to Aubrey Mellor who directed the play in Melbourne and Sydney and again with a new cast in Brisbane. He choreographed the movement of the play with such grace, elicited some very fine performances and with passion and delicacy, revealed the heart of the drama.

Finally, to my partner James Grant and our son Jack Grant for their love and encouragement, and to Kathy and Suzie Skelton who kept me entertained for years with their stories of Sorrento – thank you.

Collingwood, October 1992

The Quest for Certainty

Aubrey Mellor

I believe Hannie Rayson's rare ability to weave plot, theme and
character together with pathos and humour makes her one of our
most valued writers.

International interest confirms that the play has a wider
relevance despite its emphasis on Australian culture. Audiences
find easy access to the play through Rayson's focus on the
family and its hold on us through love, responsibility and guilt.
The past is a strong presence in the play – it haunts the present
with memories of what one was and what one had – and indeed
the play is structured so that family past is continually compared
with family present. Many of the world's greatest plays, from
King Lear to *Three Sisters*, have a family at their centre, but
few in Australia have ever managed to weave universal themes
out of what could be called the basics of 'kitchen sink' drama.

Interestingly, there is a kitchen sink in *Hotel Sorrento*. Its
presence, in a play of debate, with many speeches which could
almost be called soliloquies, raises an important question of
acting style. Some critics have referred to the work as being
naturalistic, and indeed at first glance the play appears so.
However, nothing could be further from the truth. In seeking out
a naturalness in the presentation of the delicate and exacting
scenes, an actor must beware of any naturalistic approach to the
playing as the significance of the play could easily disappear
into incident, theme and drama quickly lost in slice-of-life blur.
In approaching a production of this work, an analysis of
Rayson's succinct thematic detailing should lead to a style
which presents, almost as in Rondo musical form, a careful

exposition of its themes, then balances the repeats, transpositions and variations on these ideas, while always moving strongly through their development. Rhythm, as in most plays, is very important here – in the precision of the abundant comedy, in the exact placing and echoing of information and ideas and, particularly, in the juxtaposition of short scenes to form larger, unified movements.

The question of style is made all the more difficult because the playwright delights in the same approach to life and art as her character, the writer Meg, who proclaims the implied female perspective on the value of contradiction. 'If you don't allow yourself to see the contradictions in things', Meg says, 'your perceptions are totally blunted.' This theme becomes the playwright's form. Contradictions abound in *Hotel Sorrento*. Australian writing, for example, is criticised in the play as being 'hampered by an obsession with the vernacular'; yet at the same time the play itself is full of vernacular. Meg claims that Australia 'is a country which honours ordinariness'. Dick interprets this as an expatriate's put-down of our intellect, Marge thinks of it as an appreciation of the heroism of ordinary people, while the audience is encouraged toward another reading – a reason for our cutting down of tall poppies. All these readings are valid, and all should be given weight in the playing. It is extremely important that a production embrace this exciting approach. Much drama lies in the tension between these contradictory viewpoints.

Rayson goes further than simply setting up contradictory ideas against each other; she has created an essentially dramatic approach to characterisation. Her characters, like Chekhov's, can only be understood through an appreciation of their internal contradictions. Again, these contradictions should be embraced, not blunted. The 'quest for certainty', Meg claims, is the 'one true emblem of masculinity' and any attempt to encapsulate *Hotel Sorrento* into a statement of Ibsenesque pith will be thwarted by the many themes which vie for supremacy.

Rayson's appreciation of the value of contradiction leads us to wider perspectives.

The playwright's technique is to begin from a point of deceptive obviousness. Like Meg with her novel, Rayson has deliberately written her play to be 'accessible to ordinary people'. Its promotion of Australian arts, for example, is immediately grasped by audiences of all ages. 'Why do Australians always have to be so obvious?' asks Meg, and her playwright bravely goes on to use cultural clichés to make obvious points onto which she weaves much more subtle material.

This technique extends into characterisation. Almost all of the characters are 'types' – and I suppose one can say that about all characters in dramatic literature – yet each has unique qualities. Their surfaces are immediately recognisable and encourage instant communication with audiences, then, with often surprising twists and about-turns, the playwright continues throughout to reveal other depths. The silly Pom with the tea-cosy on his head reveals an unconditional love – rare in characterisation – and, in performance, this role can develop tragic proportions. A hard-edged, New York advertising executive has within her a frightened little girl, forever competing for the attention of her older sisters. A big-boned, outspoken feminist, insensitive to her teenage nephew, has a self-analysis that is both admirable and obsessive and a centre that is fragile and lonely. This layering of contrasts requires important and exact focus from the actors.

It is significant that a work of art is the catalyst for most of what happens in *Hotel Sorrento*; Rayson believes in the power of art to transform. This is both thematic and dramatic. The play explores this idea by exploding the worlds of all the characters with a single novel. The important 'observer' characters, as well as being participants in the action, represent the reader, viewer or audience affected by being exposed to a work of art. We see this most clearly in Marge. She argues that art need not be about huge concepts; it can find meaning in the small, the ordinary

and the parochial. Her wonderful account of the effect on her of
Helen Garner's book *Monkey Grip* highlights how Australians
have embraced their own culture in the last twenty years. For
Marge, that novel gave meaning to Fitzroy: 'This is the place
where I live and I've never seen it like this before... She gave
it to me. She gave it life.' Here, Rayson links her themes of
ordinariness with those of ownership. It is as if a true ownership
of the ordinary transforms it into the extraordinary.

This theme of ownership is very important in the play –
Rayson clearly uses the family as a metaphor for Australia – just
as the family members must face up to their past and own what
has happened to them before any reconciliation is possible, so
must we as a nation. Hilary comforts her son with the promise
that one day they will be able to say, 'This is what happened'
and have the courage to own what has happened in their lives.
In this way, the play is a contribution to our analysis of
ourselves and urges an ownership, warts and all, without the
cringe that we are not good enough and without the illusion that
we are better that others.

With this ownership comes responsibility. The play debates
issues of loyalty and truth and asks: to what degree should we
accept or criticise the faults of our loved ones and our country?
The play started as a study of expatriates and this perspective
remains strong. Meg suffers the conflicting emotions of a love-
hate relationship with her country and family. The controversial
aspect of her novel is her attack on the male-dominated culture.
Yet, ironically, the country she has refused to live in for ten
years is also the life-source of her work. Her recurring
nightmare – one shared with Troy – is that she turned her back.
To own is to face truth and accept responsibility.
It is very interesting that the 'brutalising male culture of
Australia' can produce such admirable and fascinating women.
The Moynihan sisters each have an extraordinary set of qualities
that are hugely appealing. Individually they are interesting
enough; combined they form a unit of immense attraction – one
can easily grasp Gary's dilemma! Yet all three are ordinary,

familiar, Australian women, and the daughters of the classic chauvinist Wal – 'a bastard to our mother, hopeless father' – and an oppressed, lonely woman who whinged and nagged. The past is both idealised and terrifying in *Hotel Sorrento* – in many ways a true evocation of the fifties. However, it is the ghost of the mother – who waited on the men who used her house as a hotel – that haunts the absolute centre of the play. Her daughters have to find themselves through this haunting. I need not express here the important contribution *Hotel Sorrento* makes to the feminist movement, except to observe that in encouraging ownership of what has happened, Hannie Rayson moves us into the nineties, still fiercely proclaiming the strengths of women while gently encouraging reconciliation.

The four men's roles are all supportive ones and this is rare enough in the theatre as to be remarked upon by the male actors – suddenly they understand what female actors have been saying for years. However, each one is deeply rewarding and sympathetically drawn. One husband, one friend, one father, one son; such is the playwright's fair representation of the male. Despite the fact that he is the butt of many jokes, the steady Edwin, with his final terrible choice between country and wife, is a character that women in the audience respond to most warmly. Dick for all his inability to understand women, has an integrity that invites enormous admiration. Like many committed to social justice above material wealth, he has suddenly found himself in a different world. His last scene, in which he clumsily and almost unconsciously attempts to elicit some interest from Hilary, can be one of the play's most touching. He too suffers an Australian's inability to express passion – another of the playwright's themes. Wal cannot tell his daughters that he loves them, yet now that he has mellowed it is clear that he does. Did he ever tell his wife? Troy, an excellent and demanding role for a young actor, is the touchstone of any production. His growing need to know and understand links dramatic tension beneath the surfaces.

In preparing *Hotel Sorrento* for three different performance spaces, I learned that the play benefits from a multi-purpose set which keeps many of the characters onstage almost all of the time. This not only allows the action to flow swiftly and seamlessly, but importantly allows the audience to better reflect on the resonances between the scenes. However, the text is extremely atmospheric and, with many actors onstage held in waiting moods, it becomes important that the acting never becomes melancholy. It is also important, I believe, to avoid too much naturalistic detail in the design and to trust the indicators inherent in the text.

Hannie Rayson's personal attributes and intelligent dedication make her one of the most rewarding writers to work with – her practical years in theatre are tangible assets. I thank John Gaden's devotion to her work which brought this play to my attention and to Carrillo Gantner who offered me the quickly-seized opportunity to direct it. In workshopping this material through to performance, my care was always to keep the huge and varied canvas intact and not to lose any of its richness – my thanks are due to David Berthold's assistance and to Wayne Harrison who encouraged the final cuts.

Brisbane, November, 1992.

Hotel Sorrento was first performed by the Playbox Theatre Company at the Merlyn Theatre, C.U.B. Malthouse, Melbourne on 27 July, 1990 with the following cast:

HILARY	Elspeth Ballantyne
MARGE	Julia Blake
WAL	Robin Cuming
DICK	Peter Curtin
MEG	Caroline Gillmer
EDWIN	David Latham
TROY	Tamblyn Lord
PIPPA	Genevieve Picot

Directed by Aubrey Mellor
Designed by Jennie Tate
Lighting by John Comeadow
Sound by Stuart Greenbaum

SETTING

The play takes place in the present time.
In Act One, there are three households – Meg and Edwin's flat in London, the Moynihan family home in Sorrento and Marge's holiday house in Sorrento.
In Act Two, all action takes place in Sorrento.

Sorrento is a pretty coastal town on the Mornington Peninsula in Victoria, Australia.

CHARACTERS

MARGE MORRISEY is fifty-seven, a teacher, divorcee and mother of four. All of her children have grown up and left home. She has a holiday house in Sorrento, where she goes every weekend.

DICK BENNETT, forty-three, the editor of the *Australian Voice*. His friendship with Marge dates back to the early seventies. He lives alone in a rented flat, and is a regular visitor to Marge's holiday house.

HILARY MOYNIHAN, is the eldest of the Moynihan sisters. She lives in Sorrento, in the family home, with her father and sixteen-year-old son. Her husband was killed in a car accident. She owns a small gourmet deli in the main street.

WAL MOYNIHAN, is sixty-nine, father to Hilary, Pippa and Meg. He is retired now, having been the proprietor of the local garage, Moynihan Motors. His family has been in Sorrento for generations, and as a result he is something of a local character.

TROY MOYNIHAN, Hilary's son.

EDWIN BATES, forty-five, an Englishman married to Meg. He is a partner in a successful publishing firm in London.

MEG MOYNIHAN, the middle sister, is a novelist and expatriate. She has been in London for ten years. Her second novel, *Melancholy*, has been nominated for the Booker prize.

PIPPA MOYNIHAN, is the youngest sister, currently living in New York. She is well travelled and now a highly paid advertising executive.

ACT ONE

SCENE ONE

Two figures sit on the end of the jetty. It is dusk. The man is fishing. There is remnants of fish and chips in white paper lying between them. She is reading Melancholy. *He is staring out to sea.*

MARGE: Listen,
    'In the autumn, the dusk fell gently. She sat at the end of the jetty listening to the tinkling of the masts and the water lapping at the poles. The jetty creaked at the joints and the boats bobbed about, deserted now. There was a nip in the air.
    With the demise of summer, the town seemed to settle back on itself, to mellow. The breeze no longer carried the crackle of transistors, the call of gulls and the smell of fish and chips. With the summer visitors gone, there was a sense of quiet industry about the place. It was the business of getting on with things. Across at the pier the local kids were reeling in their lines. They would go up for tea shortly, squeeze in around their kitchen tables and tuck into hot corned beef and apple sponge.
    From where she sat, she could see the quiet little foreshore with its white bandstand framed by Norfolk pine. Beyond that, the road swept up the hill into the township. She could see the rooves of the cottages, peeping out from amidst the straggle of ti-tree. She focussed on the tip of the tallest pine and counted across from the left. A red, a green, a red. The second red roof on the hill. "That's us", she whispered, and it was then that she felt it; the sweet pensive sadness, the

melancholy, the yearning for something that she could not
name.'
    [MARGE *closes the book and looks up at* DICK *expectantly.
She scrutinises his face for a response.*]
DICK: What?
MARGE: This is the jetty, I'm sure of it.
    [DICK *smirks unconvinced.*]
Look, the bandstand, the pines, the road sweeping up to the
township. Everything. It's exactly as she describes it. It's
Sorrento.

SCENE TWO

It is seven a.m. HILARY *stands on the balcony looking out to
sea. She wraps her cardigan round her tightly and holds on to
her mug of tea. She watches affectionately as her father,* WAL
and son, TROY *come up the path.* WAL *strides forward with his
towel slung over a shoulder.* TROY *scrambles behind huddled in
his towel, shivering.*

HIL: How was it?
WAL: Beautiful.
    [HIL *laughs at her son, who is standing at the bottom of
the verandah steps shivering and shaking his head to get
the water out of his ears.*]
WAL: Look at it will you. Looks like a plucked chook.
TROY: Get off!
WAL: Go on. Get into a hot shower.
HIL: Get the sand off first.
    [TROY *disappears around the back of the house.* WAL
leans on the balcony.]
WAL: Look at that, eh? It's beautiful down there this morning.
Clear as crystal that water. You ought to come with us.
    [HIL *gives him a 'don't be stupid' look. He picks up a
coat lying on a chair.*]
WAL: What's this?

HIL: It's Pip's.

WAL: Got more clothes than I've had hot breakfasts, that girl. Got a cup of tea on the go?

HIL: Mm hm.

WAL: She still asleep?

HIL: Yep.

WAL: I'll take one into her.

HIL: No, don't. Let her sleep.

WAL: Ah. . . missing the best part of the morning.

HIL: Dad. Let her sleep. They knock you about those long flights.

WAL: Yeah. S'ppose so. Bloody long time to be cooped up in one of those things.

HIL: You know she's only going to be staying for a week, don't you?

WAL: Yeah. I know, I know.

HIL: She's got to go to Melbourne.

WAL: Beats me why anyone would want to spend time in that stinkin' joint. Wouldn't get me up there if you paid me.

HIL: Yeah. Well that's why she's home. They're paying her.

[WAL *says nothing, then breaks into an indulgent smile.*]

WAL: She's glad to be home, eh? I knew she would be. Well . . . better get a wriggle on. I promised Lorna Watson I'd clean out her guttering.

HIL: Oh, Dad! What about her son-in-law? Lazy bugger. Why can't he do it?

WAL: Oh, he's got a crook back or some other bloody thing.

[*Pause*]

HIL: I was thinking, we need a coat of paint on this place.

[*She pulls a flake of paint off the wall.*]

Look at this.

WAL: Yeah. Thought we might get Tracker Johnston to give us a hand. I got a few tins of that red paint left. That oughta do us for the roof.

HIL: Yeah. I've always liked the red. Looks nice when you're looking up from the jetty.

WAL: Mm. Bit o' colour on the hill.

SCENE THREE

A London flat. Evening. MEG *opens the door to find* EDWIN *in the kitchen making a cup of tea. He has the tea cosy on his head.*

MEG: Edwin!
EDWIN: Ah, Meg, you're home.
   [*She stares at him, a smile playing on her lips.*]
   Well, you know what they say. Leave an Englishman alone in a room with a tea cosy . . .
   [MEG *goes over and kisses him.*]
MEG: Actually, it's terribly becoming.
EDWIN: Thank you. You've had twelve telephone calls.
MEG: Oh, god.
EDWIN: The price, my dear, of becoming suddenly enormously famous. I have during the course of the evening developed an overwhelming empathy with Dennis Thatcher.
   [*She holds up a scotch bottle on the table.*]
MEG: So I see. Poor you.
EDWIN: How was the new Aussie play?
MEG: Awful.
EDWIN: Oh, dear.
MEG: Why do Australians always have to be so obvious?
   [*Pause*]
   Am I obvious?
EDWIN: Let me see. . . 'Hello, how are you, would you like to have sex here, or at my place in Fulham. I don't mean to appear hasty but if you do want to have sex in Fulham we'll have to go now because the number fifteen leaves in ten minutes.' I don't know. Would you call that 'obvious'?
MEG: I never said that.
EDWIN: Perhaps not in those exact words. . .
MEG: I never lived in Fulham.

EDWIN: Ah, Chelsea. I beg your pardon.

MEG: Probably some other girl.

EDWIN: Probably.

    [*Pause*]

MEG: Anyway, you needed a bit of prodding.

EDWIN: Englishmen are notoriously coy about things of this nature.

MEG: Backward. Let's face it. Anyway I'm not talking about that. I'm talking about my book. When you read it did you think, 'God that is so obvious!'

EDWIN: No. Why?

MEG: I was beginning to wonder whether it was a cultural handicap.

EDWIN: Being obvious?

MEG: Yes.

EDWIN: Well let's face it, you lot like to call a spade a spade, don't you, which is all very admirable in real life. . . but if you think about it, it doesn't make for great drama does it?

    [MEG *looks at him curiously.*]

Well take *Hamlet*. An Australian could never have written that. You'd have Hamlet walking on stage saying, 'Cut the bullshit. I don't believe in ghosts'. And the whole thing would've been over in a couple of minutes.

    [MEG *is only vaguely listening. She is flipping through some mail on the table.*]

You see, I think as a people you appear to be very suspicious of subtext actually.

MEG: Jesus, Edwin.

EDWIN: It has something to do with an unwillingness to deal with the emotional texture of things.

MEG: Really?

EDWIN: Mmm. It's like the English chatter on ad nauseam and quite inadvertently we blunder into revealing things about ourselves. But your lot seem to do either of two things. They say exactly what's going on. Or else they're dead silent. Oh, no, there's a third thing. They do a lot of grunting. The men.

[MEG *laughs despite herself.*]

So it's not like Australians are less complex emotionally. .

MEG: Oh, Edwin. . .

EDWIN: Well I used to think it was. I thought that was why I was so attracted to them – being so inordinately repressed myself as a human being – but I've realised it's all to do with the way it's expressed. You see, if you take. . .

MEG: Who was on the phone?

EDWIN: Have a look. There's the list. Journalists mostly.

MEG: What are they doing ringing me on a Friday night?

[EDWIN *shrugs*]

EDWIN: Nothing much on the telly I s'ppose.

[*Pause*]

One chap rang from Australia. He said he used to go out with your sister.

MEG: Which one?

EDWIN: Pippa.

MEG: That's hardly a claim to fame.

EDWIN: That's what I said to him. 'You and the rest of the male population'.

MEG: You didn't!

EDWIN: I did.

MEG: What did he want?

EDWIN: Same as everybody else. An exclusive. The Meg Moynihan story. The unknown Aussie novelist makes it to the Booker short list with her second novel.

[MEG *sighs and briefly scans the letter she is holding.*]

MEG: Jesus Christ!

[*She flings it on the table.*]

EDWIN: What is it?

MEG: The London Book Council. They're organising a forum on women and autobiography. They want me to give the opening address.

EDWIN: What do you know about autobiography?

MEG: Exactly.

    [*Pause*]

But you must understand, I'm a woman writer. And as such I don't have any frame of reference beyond my own immediate experience. Didn't you know all novels written by women are merely dressed up diary entries?

EDWIN: So your novel is *really* about the adventures of Meg Moynihan en famille. That's quite funny really.

MEG: Hilarious.

EDWIN: I wonder what your sisters would make of that?

MEG: They'd think it was ridiculous. Do you know, at that play tonight, Carmel refused to speak during the interval in case anyone recognised her accent. I can't tell you how much that irritated me.

EDWIN: I would have thought it was quite affirming for you. Seeing something really bad. Then you can say to yourself - isn't it good. I don't live there any more.

    [*Pause*]

MEG: Edwin, where did you get that shirt?

EDWIN: I bought it at the Camden market on Sunday. Seventy-five p. Not bad eh?

MEG: I think you got ripped off.

SCENE FOUR

HILARY *is ironing. From the ashtray placed on one end of the ironing board we see a single stream of blue smoke.* TROY *is sitting at the kitchen table reading the paper.* PIP *enters looking decidedly the worse for wear. However, despite her dishevelled appearance she looks stylish in her silk robe.*

HIL: Ah. . . good afternoon.

PIP: What time is it?

HIL: Eleven.

PIP: Oh, is that all. My tongue feels like it's got a sock on it. Did we drink a huge amount last night or am I imagining things?

TROY: About a dozen stubbies, half a dozen bottles of champagne and then you two got stuck into the whisky.

HIL: Thank you Troy.

PIP: You're kidding?

HIL: Yes. He's kidding. [*To* TROY] Put the kettle on Troy.

[*He leans over and plugs it in.*]

PIP: Not for me. [*He pulls the plug out.*] I think I'll just sit for a minute.

[*Pause*]

Why aren't you at the deli?

HIL: Well, it's not every day that your little sister comes home.

PIP: You know no-one over there drinks much these days. Not in New York anyway. I'm out of practice. What are you grinning about?

TROY: Nothing.

[HILARY *plonks a glass of water down in front of her and an aspro.*]

HIL: Probably jet lag.

TROY: I doubt it.

HIL: Put the kettle on Troy.

[*He puts the plug back in.*]

PIP: Ugh, that cigarette stinks. [*Disapprovingly*] You're still smoking Hil.

HIL: No Pip. I gave it away. [*To her son, warning against further nagging*] And don't you start.

TROY: Did I say anything?

[HILARY *makes a face at her son.*]

[*Pause*]

PIP: Is that old thing still going? [*Indicating the iron*]

HIL: Mm hmm.

PIP: I thought so. Poor old Mum. Outlived by her iron.

[*Pause*]

Yeah. Life sucks, when you think about it. What d'you reckon Troy?

TROY: Mm hm.

HIL: Troy?

TROY: What?

HIL: She just proffered an extremely contentious philosophical point of view. You don't just say mm hm.

TROY: Why not?

HIL: Well you either agree or disagree . . .

TROY: I agree.

HIL: You do not. You're sixteen years old. When you're sixteen years old life does not suck. Life is. . . brimming with. . . excitement and. . . purpose. Isn't it Pippa?

[PIP *giggles*]

TROY: She can't remember.

PIP: I can so.

[*Pause*]

HIL: Poor ol' Mum.

PIP: She'd be here night after night on her own, wouldn't she? Always got the rough end of the stick, our Mum.

TROY: Where was Pop?

PIP: Out fishing.

HIL: Or in the pub. But mostly they'd be out in the bay. Dad and Ernie Mac, Tracker Johnson, Jock Farrell. All that lot.

PIP: Mick Hennessey.

HIL: He wouldn't get in till after midnight some nights. Remember? We'd hear him coming down the hall, banging against the walls. He'd throw the fish in the sink and crash into bed. Drunk as a skunk.

PIP: Yeah.

HIL: It's cruel I reckon.

[*Pause*]

PIP: What do you mean?

HIL: Well he was a bastard to our mother. Hopeless father, all of that. But when it all boils down, he's the one that everyone loves. We all love him. Don't we?

PIP: Yeah.

HIL: More than we ever loved her. [PIP *looks dubious.*] It's true.
And yet she was the one that kept it all together.

> [*Silence. The flywire screen door slaps. They exchange
> looks, hoping their father didn't overhear.* WAL *enters. He
> is carrying a bag of fish.*]

WAL: Ah, you're up?

PIP: Yeah.

WAL: Good. Ernie Mac gave us a few flatties. He said to say
g'day by the way.

PIP: Oh, yeah.

WAL: Thought we might scrub 'em up for tea. What d'ya
reckon?

PIP: Beauty.

> [*He chucks them in the sink. The others smile at the
> sound.*]

WAL: What are you laughin' at?

PIP: Nothing.

HIL: Don't look at me. I'm not gonna clean 'em.

WAL: All right. No-one's askin' ya. [*He grins.*] Troy here's not
doin' anythin.

> [TROY *makes a face.*]

TROY: No. I'm just sitting here brimming with life and purpose.

> [*The girls burst out laughing.*]

HIL: What do you do with a kid like that?

> [*The kettle starts whistling.*]

WAL: What's that kettle doin'. Turn it off will ya.

> [TROY *leans over and pulls the plug out again, shaking
> his head.*]

TROY: I don't believe this.

> [PIPPA *laughs and leans over ruffling his hair
> affectionately.*]

WAL: Well. . . I got a bit more news. [*He pulls a little piece of
torn up newspaper from his pocket.*] Last Thursdy's *Herald.*
I was up at Lorna Watson's.

PIP: Lorna Watson? God. She still alive?

WAL: Yeah. An' doing very nicely if you don't mind. Any rate, she was sayin', 'Wal, those girls of yours have done very well for 'emselves'.

HIL: Meaning you and Meg.

WAL: Nah. Come on. Meaning all of yous. What with you [PIP] bein' in the States makin' more money than Rupert Murdoch . . .

PIP: Yeah, come on, get on with it.

WAL: And Meg winnin' that book prize.

PIP: She hasn't won it yet Dad.

WAL: Yeah, I know. Still . . .Any rate we got talkin' and she showed me this. [*He opens out the piece torn from the paper and hands it to* TROY.] I haven't got me glasses. Read it out will you Troy.

TROY: 'AAP. London. Expatriate Australian novelist Meg Moynihan has been nominated for the prestigious Booker McConnell Prize. Her novel *Melancholy* was included on the shortlist announced yesterday. With literary heavyweights like Fredrico Kutz. . .

PIP: Koetz.

TROY: Koetz, and Johnathon Drewmore as contenders, insiders are speculating that a win for the Australian seems unlikely.

HIL: Sounds like a horse race.

WAL: Ssh. Go on.

PIP: They take bets on it you know.

HIL: Bullshit.

PIP: They do.

TROY: You right?

WAL: Come on. Get on with it.

TROY: 'Moynihan's novel, which deals with the rites of passage of a young woman living in an isolated coastal town in the fifties, is a contentious choice. Her central argument is that in the brutalising male culture of Australia in the fifties, a woman's survival was conditional on the extent to which she was prepared to betray her sisters.'

[TROY *pauses momentarily. An awkward silence descends.*]

'The novel has been described as displaying a disappointing lack of stylistic ambition by London critics whereas Lucinda Brampton of *The New York Book Review* hailed it as containing one of the most exquisitely executed scenes of recent English language fiction.'

[TROY *looks up.*]

HIL: Is that it?

TROY: Mm hm.

WAL: Not bad, eh? [*To* PIP] Never thought your own sister'd be a celebrity did you? Eh?

PIP: Yeah. I knew.

HIL: [*to* WAL] I reckon you're the one that's most surprised. It would never have entered your head that a daughter of yours'd be anything out of the bag.

PIP: Well you gotta admit, 'being a daughter of his', that's the weird part. [*They laugh.*]

SCENE FIVE

MARGE *and* DICK *on the jetty.* MARGE *is looking at the cover of the book lovingly. She is obviously quite transported by it.*

MARGE: *Melancholy.* Such a lovely title. [*Sighing*] And to think that you hated it.

DICK: I didn't hate it. I told you, I just find it hard to believe that it's been nominated for the Booker prize. I mean it's all right: a very nice, sentimental, lightweight piece of fiction. A good read, all that stuff, but it's certainly not great literature.

MARGE: You know what I think? I think that melancholy is something that men don't understand. Australian men, dare I say it.

DICK: Bullshit.

MARGE: No. You confuse it with depression. Which is different. See, I know exactly what she's talking about. There are certain times when I feel overcome by this immense sadness. But it isn't depressing. It's tender and gentle. . . I don't know how to describe it. . . It's very female, I think.

DICK: Is this before you went through the change, Marge?

MARGE: Don't be cheeky, you! [DICK *laughs*] Anyway, what's great literature supposed to be? If I may be so bold as to seek definition? — *Sarcasm*.

DICK: Great literature. Let me see. Great literature awakens us to our humanity. Like fishing. [*He chuckles.* MARGE *rolls her eyes.*] It certainly isn't about gender politics, that's for sure.

MARGE: This isn't about gender politics.

DICK: Ah, but you're trying to explain my indifference by arguing that I can't really appreciate its true worth because I'm a man.

MARGE: Not because you're a man, my dear. Merely that you have blunted sensitivities. Obviously.

DICK: No. Don't wheedle your way out of it. 'Men don't experience melancholy'. That's what you said.

MARGE: Well. Do you?

DICK: Yes. I do, as a matter of fact. And I have. [*He smirks.*] When I've been feeling particularly self indulgent.

MARGE: Ah, why do we women bother?

DICK: I didn't think you did.

MARGE: Well that's true. 'Cept for a few old mates. How long have we known each other?

DICK: Footscray High. Staffroom. '72.

MARGE: Twenty years. Tsch. Long time to have a friendship when you don't share the same sensibilities. What do you think is the basis of it?

[DICK *shrugs. They are both smirking.*]

DICK: The Cause?

MARGE: Which neither of us is committed to any more.

DICK: Well, I wouldn't say that. We've just 'modified' our political thinking haven't we?

[MARGE *laughs.*]
Maybe it's to do with the fact that you have a weekender in Sorrento which I'm rather fond of visiting.

MARGE: Oh, don't say that.

DICK: You should know about the folly of acquiring property.

MARGE: Hmph. A place where the ideologues can come and enjoy the view with a clear conscience.

[DICK *laughs.*]
Anyway, what happened about that house you were going to buy?

DICK: Oh, I think I missed the boat, somewhere along the line Marge.

MARGE: Tsch. Forty-two years of age and you're still living in student digs.

DICK: Forty-three actually.

[*Pause*]

[*Her tone becomes more serious.*]

MARGE: You've invested quite a lot in the paper haven't you?

DICK: With its circulation dropping at a rate of knots every week. [*Silence*] Australians don't really want to hear an independent voice telling them that they're being duped. But I suppose any fool could have told me that.

SCENE SIX

The kitchen. TROY *is doing his maths homework on the table.* PIPPA *is sitting on the stool.* HILARY *is reading.*

PIP: Have you heard from Meg recently?

HIL: Not for a while.

PIP: Do you write?

HIL: Of course.

[*Pause*]

PIP: Bloody awful title, *Melancholy.* She needs a marketing manager.

HIL: She doesn't seem to be doing too badly.

PIP: I suppose it could've been worse. She could've called it 'Depression'.

TROY: I think it's a good title.

HIL: Concentrate on your homework Troy.

PIP: [*looking over at* HIL's *book quizzically*] What *are* you reading? *The Canterbury Tales*?

HIL: Mmm hmm.

PIP: Chaucer! At your age?

HIL: Thank you.

PIP: Oh, well, no accounting for taste is there Troy?

   [*Pause*]

   I'm thinking of coming back at the end of the year.

HIL: Really?

PIP: Mmm. My contract finishes in December. I mean I could renew it, but. . . I dunno.

HIL: What about Martin?

   [PIP *shrugs.*]

   Oh, Pip. I thought it was serious between you two.

PIP: Yeah. . . so did I. But it doesn't seem like anyone wants to take me *that* seriously.

HILARY: What do you mean?

PIP: Well, I'm kind of. . . entertainment value, but not a serious contender.

   [*Pause*]

   He wants a nice Jewish girl.

HIL: I thought he'd come to terms with that.

PIP: Yeah. He has. He found a nice Jewish girl.

HIL: Oh, no Pip.

   [PIP *shrugs.*]

PIP: If it wasn't that, it'd be something else.

   [*Pause*]

   It always is.

   [*Pause*]

   Did I tell you about going to visit his parents?

HIL: No.

PIP: I was so nervous I dropped a lump of mozzarella cheese into the fish tank.

HIL: Oh, no.

[WAL *enters*]

PIP: Yeah. And I'm not just talking about a little lump of cheese. This thing was huge. When it went in, the water went out in a big way. . . along with about fifty tropical fish. They kind of dived onto the carpet. All I can remember is turning around and seeing Martin's Mum standing on a chair screeching 'Get the cat out'.

HIL: Oh, I am sorry Pip. . .

PIP: Yeah, things seemed to take a turn for the worse after that.

[*Silence*]

WAL: You're a silly bugger.

SCENE SEVEN

MEG *is sitting on the lounge room floor reading aloud excerpts from a letter from* HILARY.

MEG: Listen to this bit. . .

EDWIN: This is still from Hilary?

MEG: Yeah. . . [*She reads aloud.*] 'I'm doing an English course with the Council of Adult Education. We are studying Chaucer at the moment. It's very interesting.'

See what I mean? Chaucer is not interesting. Chaucer is very, very dull.

EDWIN: So, she finds it interesting.

MEG: She does not. She just thinks she *should* find it interesting, because that's what being 'cultured' is all about.

EDWIN: Being conversant with things that are irrelevant and dull.

MEG: Exactly. That's what the whole middle class is like back home. They go off and memorise Shakespeare's date of birth and a few rhyming couplets so they can sprinkle it in conversation around the barbie. 'D'you think Kylie'll bring the coleslaw.' 'Ah, To bring or not to bring. That is the question. Shakespeare you know. Born in 1564, strangely enough.' 'Yes. Died in 1616. Poor thing. Such a tragedy. Terrific bean salad Val.'

EDWIN: Ooh, you're such a snob.

MEG: No, I'm not. I don't care two hoots about Shakespeare, you know that. In fact I've often thought that my idea of purgatory would be an everlasting subscription to the Royal Shakespeare Company.

place of punishment (not heaven or hell) in between

EDWIN: I'll never forget the look on Peter Hall's face, the night you told him that you thought *Othello* was dreadfully overwritten.

MEG: Ah you see, that's one thing I really regret about ageing. I resent having to mellow. I'd never say that sort of thing now.

EDWIN: Well, that's just as well I should think. I can just see *The Times Literary Supplement*. Booker prize nominee Meg Moynihan says that Shakespeare's plays are dreadfully overwritten.

MEG: But that's what it's like at home. For all that obsessive nationalism, people still equate 'culture' with Shakespeare and Chaucer.

[*Pause.* MEG *sighs*]

I just wish she'd say something about my book. [*She wrinkles up her nose.*] It's silly isn't it, 'cause on one level I don't give a damn what she thinks of it – as a piece of 'literature.' I just want a reaction. Anything. 'Dear Meg, I found your book excruciatingly turgid.'

EDWIN: Maybe she hasn't read it yet. Too busy swatting up on Chaucer.

[*Pause*]

MEG: If you'd written a book, you'd expect your family to read it wouldn't you?

EDWIN: Oh, not necessarily. I suspect the last book that Gareth ever read was probably *Biggles*. Might be expecting too much.

[*Pause*]

MEG: I bet she has read it. She's just not saying anything.

[*Pause.* EDWIN *looks at her appraisingly. She looks away. Pause.*]

She says. . . 'You'll be pleased to hear that Dad is much better. I think the fact that Pip is arriving has cheered him enormously'. [*She sighs*] Why does she always do this ?

EDWIN: What?

MEG: Oh, make me feel so damn guilty about everything.

SCENE EIGHT

HIL *and* PIPPA *are walking arm in arm along the jetty. They stop and lean on the railing looking out across the bay, oblivious to the couple at the end of the jetty.*

PIP: D'you remember the time I drank Mum's liquid foundation?

HIL: That was Oil of Ulan wasn't it?

PIP: No. It was brown. I think I must have thought it was chocolate milk.

HIL: Poor ol' Mum. She'd probably saved up for months to buy that stuff. And then her daughter drinks it.

PIP: God. I must have been seriously defective. Why did you take the blame for it?

HIL: I didn't. Meg did.

PIP: Meg? I thought it was you. You told Mum you spilt it in the basin.

HIL: No. Meg took the blame.

PIP: Really?

[*Pause*]

Why would she have done that?

HIL: I don't know.

PIP: God! She's weird that woman. [HIL *laughs.*] Well she is. That's just another example of it. It shits me.

HIL: You should write to her and tell her. 'Dear Meg, I feel compelled to tell you that I'm still deeply angry about the Liquid foundation incident in 1961.'

PIP: You don't understand.

> [*Pause*]

HIL: I do.

> [*They muse privately.*]

PIP: It's odd isn't it, all these bits and pieces turning up in Meg's book. I felt. . . cheated or something.

> [*Pause*]

> It makes me feel that my childhood, well, our childhood has been. . . sort of. . . raided. Not that anyone's going to say, 'Oh, that's Pippa' or, 'that's Hilary' or whatever, but it kind of does something to your own memories. Not that there's anything deep and meaningful in there. . . about us. . . It's just the little things. It's almost as if they're not ours any more.

> [*Pause*]

HIL: I don't care about the little things.

SCENE NINE

MARGE *and* DICK *are relaxing in easy chairs in the garden of* MARGE*'s holiday shack in Sorrento.*

MARGE: When you were growing up. . .?

DICK: Mm?

MARGE: Did you think that you were ordinary or did you think that you were special?

> [DICK *frowns and shrugs.*]

DICK: I don't know. What? You mean did I think I was going to be. . . one of the great minds of my generation?

> [MARGE *smiles.*]

> For a while there, I thought I might be a famous detective; I remember that. Then when I was about fifteen I modified it a bit and thought I might run a crime bookshop. There was this bloke who ran one of those bookshops in the city and I used to go down there with my Dad every so often. I used to think there was something really good about that

bloke. He was a complete slob. He was about fifty and he was open all weekend. He was totally into it. He had none of the trappings of the suburban shit that my family went on with. He used to chain smoke Gaulois and then he'd stub 'em out in the left overs of his Chinese take-away.

very strong.

French smokes.

MARGE: Oh, yuck.

DICK: I used to think there was something really. . . magnificent about that! It was a statement really.

MARGE: Oh, Dick!

DICK: It was! It was a statement about anarchy. And I remember reading it as such.

MARGE: Anarchy?

DICK: I thought my mother, my sisters, they'd never understand this. My mother would not be able to hold herself back. She would have to get a plastic bag and put the whole contents of his desk [his life work I might add] in the rubbish. She would have to impose her suburban mentality. She would have to stamp on this. . . this. . . simple gesture of. . .

MARGE: It didn't occur to you that the simple gesture of stubbing out the cigarette in the empty contents of his take-away. . .

DICK: It wasn't empty. It had stuff in it.

MARGE: Right. Sorry. The simple gesture of stubbing the cigarette into a container of cold, congealed, sweet and sour pork. . .

DICK: It was noodles actually.

MARGE: Noodles, OK. . . could also have been read as the act of a pathetic human being who had no grasp of the simple concept of personal hygiene, because. . . wait. . . he expected his mother or some other female figure to clean up after him. That never occurred to you?

DICK: No.

MARGE: Well there you are you see. Therein lies the great tension between feminism and the Left. [DICK *laughs*.] I would have read it very differently of course.

DICK: You would have read it like my mother, who believes there is great virtue in a clean sink.

MARGE: I agree with her.

DICK: I know you do. It's just that you've developed your personal philosophies a little more over the years, I think.

MARGE: Thank you dear. Mind you to what end I'm not so sure. Is she happy your mother?

DICK: Don't be silly. Why waste time being happy when you could be cleaning the venetians.

MARGE: You must be a great disappointment to her. That's all I can say.

DICK: That I am. It's a small achievement I know. But I've spent years working on it.

[MARGE *shakes her head. They muse.*]

MARGE: You know when I asked you before about whether you thought you were special? Listen, [MARGE *reads aloud from a section of the book. Lights come up on* HILARY, *working at her desk in her own space.*] 'There was something very ordinary about Helen. Ordinary and sensible. She had an ordinary face. People would stop her in the street. "Don't I know you from somewhere?" It used to happen a lot. She'd shimmer with pleasure, shrugging it off for our benefit of course, but inside she held on to that hard little nugget of hope that there was something distinctive about her. Something that would single her out in a crowd. A permissible vanity. After all what good would it do to know that you were indistinguishable from a thousand others. But then again, it is a country which honours ordinariness above all else. She might have taken heart that she'd always be cherished for it.'

DICK: [*nodding*] Yeah?

MARGE: That really touches me. I keep going back to it.

[*Pause*]

Do you think this is a country that honours ordinariness?

DICK: No. It might have been like that in the fifties, but not any more. See that's what irritates me about that bloody book.

There are hundreds of 'em. Every Tom, Dick and Harry's writing one. Growing up in the fifties. My childhood in Toowoomba, my tortured adolescence in Kalgoorlie, or Woy Woy or some other bloody place. And you know what it is? It is essentially culturally reactionary stuff. I mean sure, the fifties was a time when it was impossible to be . . . different . . . if you like. Anyone with any nouse packed up and cleared out. But it's not like that now. And to keep harking back to it. . . it's just very safe territory. It's not going to shake anyone up.

MARGE: It's shaken me up.

[*Pause*]

Maybe you don't read between the lines. There's nothing safe about this. . .

DICK: I despise nostalgia.

[MARGE *scoffs.*]

MARGE: It's not nostalgia.

DICK: Where are the people who are writing about the big picture. Hmm? Who's tackling the big issues? Who's trying to come to grips with some sort of contemporary vision about this place? Can you think of anyone?

MARGE: Yes, I can think of lots. But. . . Meg Moynihan comes to mind. Off the top of my head. [*She smiles.*]

DICK: Oh, Jesus!

MARGE: You're looking for the big, broad brush stroke. Aren't you? I know you are. But Australia can't be contained in the sort of broad sweep that you're asking for. Great big visions make very empty pictures if you don't attend to the details.

SCENE TEN

TROY *comes into the kitchen switching on the overhead light. He pours himself a glass of milk.*

TROY: You still at it Mum?

[*He downs the glass of milk and pours another one.*]

HILARY: Books won't balance themselves.

TROY: You know, I've been thinking. . .

HILARY: Good god.

TROY : Mum!

HILARY: Come on what were you thinking? I have an inkling that it involves money.

TROY: Yeah.

HILARY: Yeah. You know how I know. I have this involuntary sensation of my stomach kind of turning over.

TROY: Really?

HILARY: Mmm hmm.

TROY: Well you know how I know that you know?

HILARY: How?

TROY: Your lips go really thin and mean and they disappear inside your mouth.

HILARY: They do not.

TROY: They do. They make a little round hole like a chook's bum.

HILARY: That's nice. Thank you for that.

TROY: Wanna hear my idea?

HILARY: No.

TROY: I'll tell you anyway. OK. If we had a *lot* of money . . . quite a lot of money.

HILARY: Mm.

TROY: So as we could be. . . not rich. . . but. . . fairly rich.

HILARY: Come on, come on. Let's be filthy rich.

TROY: Right. We could buy a flat. In St Kilda.

HILARY: [*laughing*] I thought you hated Melbourne.

TROY: Yeah. But St.Kilda's something else.

[*Pause*]

Brett Williams' Dad's got a flat in St Kilda and it's really good.

HILARY: Has he just.

TROY: He goes every second weekend. They go to the footy and the movies and have their tea in restaurants. Stuff like that.

HILARY: His parents separated are they?

TROY: Yeah. They hate each other's guts.

HILARY: Oh, charming.

TROY: I reckon you should. . . you know, get together with Brett's Dad.

HILARY: Oh, yeah. Sure Troy.

> [*Pause*]

> What's he got to offer? Apart from the flat in St Kilda of course.

TROY: [*shrugging*] He plays a pretty mean game of golf.

HILARY: Wow, quick, get me his number.

TROY: What have you got against golf?

HILARY: I don't have anything against golf. I am just repulsed by people who play it.

TROY: Mum.

HIL: I bet he wears SLACKS. . .!?

TROY: Get out.

HILARY: You know when somebody runs their finger down a blackboard. That's the feeling that white slacks give me.

TROY: You've never even met the guy.

HILARY: I know. He's probably got a very nice personality.

TROY: Not really. He's a dickhead.

> [*They laugh.* HILARY *looks at her son, her eyes shining with affection.*]

HILARY: What would I do without you. Hey?

> [*Pause*]

TROY: I'm sort of glad you're not divorced Mum.

> [*Pause*]

> Sometimes I think it's better. . . this way.

> [HILARY *says nothing. She does not look up. There is a long pause.*]

> Brett's got this. . . stutter. Not all the time. He had to go to this shrink in Melbourne. He reckons it's because his oldies got divorced. D'you reckon that's true?

> [HILARY *shrugs. Pause*]

HILARY: Oh. . . kids bounce. That's what they say isn't it?

TROY: What d'you mean?

HILARY: They cope. Sometimes I think they cope better than adults. Look at you. You've coped. But maybe it's different for you because your father's dead. Sometimes I wonder whether a death isn't easier to deal with. Because it's final. And because it's nobody's fault. I don't know, Troy.

[*Pause. Her tone lightens.*]

If things'd been different and your oldies had got divorced, never know what might have happened to you. Might have been a dribbler. That'd be nasty.

[TROY *does not respond to the joke. There is an awkward pause.* HILARY *lights a cigarette.*]

It was only a joke.

TROY: Yeah. Well it wasn't very funny.

HILARY: Sorry.

TROY: How come you can't be serious.

HILARY: About what?

[*Pause*]

TROY: Have you read Aunt Meg's book?

HILARY: [*snapping*] What made you think of that?

TROY: I dunno.

HILARY: I mean how come you said that, Troy? Just out of the blue, like that?

TROY: I don't know.

[*Pause*]

Have you read it?

HILARY: Yes. I've read it.

TROY: Do you mind if I read it?

HILARY: No. Why should I mind?

[*Pause*]

I didn't think you'd be interested.

[*Silence*]

TROY : 'Course I'm interested.

HILARY: Well read it then. [HILARY *gathers up her book work.*] I'm going to bed. Good night. [*She kisses him lightly on the forehead.* TROY *stands alone in the kitchen, looking disgruntled.*]

SCENE ELEVEN

Exterior, London flat. MEG *storms up the stairs to their flat,* EDWIN *in tow.*

MEG: 'Ors-tralians are just like their country. Big and empty.' Ha! Ha! That is the last time, Edwin. He is a pompous old bore and I'm not going to put up with it.

EDWIN: He was only trying to get a rise out of you.

MEG: Well he succeeded.

EDWIN: Oh, come on Meg. He's seventy-one.

MEG: Since when was age ever an excuse for anything. Anyway, it's not only your father. What about Gareth? He's as bad as that other little prick you work with. 'We used to dread arriving at parties too early. Imagine being the only one there in a room full of Or-stralians.'

EDWIN: Well, Gareth's a prick. That's well documented. . .but Dad doesn't mean any harm.

> [MEG *is rooting around in her handbag for the keys to the flat.*]

MEG: He's so fucking patronising towards me.

EDWIN: Look, I've told you. Dad's like that with everyone. Either tell him you find all this Australian rubbish he goes on with. . . offensive. Or else quit being so sensitive. It's getting tedious.

> [MEG *has tipped her handbag onto the step in search of her keys.*]

MEG: Oh, tedious is it? Well, you try being an outsider in this dump of a country and see how you like it.

EDWIN: You're hardly an outsider, Meg for godsake.

> [MEG *raises her voice.*]

MEG: How would you know what it's like?

EDWIN: Ssh..

MEG: You've never set foot off home turf for more than two weeks except for some cruddy little package holiday in Spain.

EDWIN: Sssh.

MEG: No, I will not sshhh. You have no understanding of what this is like. The minute I open my mouth I'm an outsider. There's more prejudice in this shithouse place. . .

EDWIN: Give me the keys.

MEG: No I will not!

[*She flings them on the ground.*]

EDWIN: For Chrissake Meg. You've almost been given the most prestigious bloody honour that this country could bestow on anyone and you're behaving like they've taken your sodding pension cheque away. Outsider? What rubbish! If you'd stayed in Australia you'd be a fucking school teacher.

[EDWIN *picks up the keys and proceeds to unlock the door.*]

MEG: Bullshit!

EDWIN: You've said as much yourself Meg!

MEG: That's crap.

[EDWIN *pushes the door open.*]

EDWIN: Well go home then.

[*He slams the door behind him.* MEG *sits down on the step outside. She looks up suddenly as someone is watching her from the window of the flat opposite.*]

MEG: [*yelling*] What are you looking at? Why don't you go and feed your fucking gas metres?

SCENE TWELVE

TROY *and* PIP *are fishing together on the jetty where* MARGE *and* DICK *were sitting earlier.*

TROY: Pip?

PIP: Mm?

TROY: Have you read Aunt Meg's book ?

PIP: Yeah.

TROY: What d'you think?

PIP: Have you read it?

TROY: No.

[*Pause.* PIP *looks uncomfortable.*]

PIP: Well it's good. Very well written.

[*Pause*]

I mean that's what everyone is saying. The critics and everyone.

TROY: Yeah. I mean did you like it?

PIP: Mmm. [*She takes a deep breath. Pause.*]

TROY: I read this letter that Meg sent to Mum. [*He steals a glance at* PIP. *She gives him a disapproving look.*] Yeah, I know. Anyway she said that people might think that the 'Helen' character was. . . Mum. But that she shouldn't worry because it wasn't supposed to be. . . or something like that.

PIP: What else did she say? Did she say anything about the Grace character?

[TROY *shrugs*]

TROY: Does it make Mum out to be. . . an idiot or something?

PIP: No. Nothing like that.

TROY: Well, what is it then? How come everyone just goes silent.

[*Pause*]

Is it about my Dad?

[*Long pause*]

PIP: Why don't you read it. You read it. . . and make up your own mind? It's sort of about all of us. In a way. . .

TROY: Make up my mind about what, Pip? I didn't even know him.

[*Pause*]

PIP: Yeah.

[PIP *nods sympathetically, however we sense that she is feeling deeply uncomfortable.*]

TROY: You know. . . the guys at school reckon I'm really lucky. 'Cos they reckon you can talk to my Mum about anything. All the guys I know reckon she's really ace.

PIP: She is.

TROY: Yeah. But you can't talk to her about everything. Not everything. I can't anyway. I don't even know how it

happened, Pip. I know he had a car accident. But there's
more to it than that isn't there?

[PIPPA *stares resolutely out to sea. The question lies
hanging.*]

SCENE THIRTEEN

Interior of the London flat. EDWIN *is pouring himself a scotch,
when* MEG *comes into the room.*

MEG: What do you mean by that - go home! What's that
supposed to mean?

EDWIN: Exactly that. Book yourself a flight and go home for a
while.

MEG: Oh, sure. Forget about the Booker. Just go and have a
holiday.

EDWIN: Yes.

[MEG *scoffs incredulously*]

MEG: You can't be serious. I've got to be in London till the
26th October. I've got publicity appearances lined up. . .

EDWIN: Cancel them! It's turning you into a screaming ratbag.

MEG: Oh, thank you Edwin.

EDWIN: You've said as much yourself! And you've been talking
obsessively about Australia and your family for weeks now.
Just go for a month. And then come back.

MEG: Thanks a lot for your support! [MEG *picks up the paper.*]

EDWIN: Oh, don't.

MEG: Why not?

EDWIN: It's that interview you did, and you're hardly in the
right frame of mind to read it at the moment.

[WAL *calls to* PIP *and* TROY *at the end of the jetty.*]

WAL: Pippy! Troy! Come up and get your tea.

SCENE FOURTEEN

MARGE *skips up the steps of her holiday house, carrying a string bag full of shopping. She is obviously pleased with herself.* DICK *is perusing the papers on the verandah.*

MARGE: Dick? Oh, Dick, guess what? I was right. I knew I was. I knew from the moment I read that first chapter. It's Sorrento all right! I've just been speaking to the people who run the paddle boats down on the beach during the summer. They've been here for years. I knew they'd know. And sure enough, the Moynihan family has been in Sorrento for as long as they can remember. Apparently they used to run a garage on the Back Beach road and a little cafe next door. The Neptune Cafe. So I walked back that way on my way home and blow me down, there it is. It's not used as a garage any more but you can still see the sign 'Moynihan Motors.' They have mini golf or something in there now. Isn't that incredible. I'm so thrilled. I can't tell you.

DICK: Are they still here?

MARGE: The old man apparently and one daughter. She runs the deli in the main street.

DICK: Oh, yeah.

MARGE: But Meg, the writer, she lives in London, of course.

DICK: Yes. I know. She did an interview with *The Guardian* recently.

MARGE: Oh.

[DICK *takes out a sheet of paper from his briefcase. He hands it to her.*]

DICK: Special delivery for you. Hot off the fax from work.

MARGE: Oh, thanks.

DICK: Mm. I'll be interested to hear what you think, but as far as I'm concerned she sounds like a pain in the arse.

SCENE FIFTEEN

The London flat. MEG *is in a state of agitation. She is waving* The Guardian *having just read a feature article about herself.*

MEG: I sound like such a pain in the arse.

EDWIN: Don't let it get to you Meg.

MEG: I tell you, that is the last time. I am never going to do another interview. Never!

EDWIN: The guy's a prat. The whole article's completely disjointed.

MEG: I'm not cut out for this. I can't stand it. All this hype and carry on. I hate it and I can't handle it any more.

[*She starts to cry.*]

EDWIN: Oh, sweetheart. Sweet heart.

MEG: My family sound like morons. What would they think if they read this at home? They'd be so angry and hurt.

EDWIN: Hey, come on. That's the one thing you don't have to worry about. Who's going to read *The Guardian* in Sorrento? Hmm? They probably don't even have it on the newsstands.

[*Long pause*]

MEG: They don't even have a newsstand.

SCENE SIXTEEN

On the verandah at MARGE*'s place. They sit drinking coffee.* MARGE *has* The Guardian *article in her lap.*

DICK: These bloody smart arse expatriates. I mean what is it that makes them think that living elsewhere automatically qualifies them to make sweeping generalisations about this place. A culture isn't static for godsake. Things change. The woman hasn't lived here for ten years. Look what's happened in that time.

MARGE: Yes, it is a bit disappointing, I have to admit.

DICK: Disappointing. Jesus! The woman's an idiot.

MARGE: No, she's not. She's not an idiot.

[DICK *scoffs.*]

DICK: I might seem like an idiot, talk like an idiot. But don't be deceived. I *am* an idiot!

MARGE: Well, I think some of the things she says are quite true. I love this bit,

'If you ask the average Brit what he knows about Australia, he'll probably say Fosters and vomit. The trouble is that your average Aussie bloke on the loose in London, regardless of whether he's backpacking or wheeling and dealing, does nothing to dispel that image. When I meet Australians over here I take some comfort in the fact that it is only a minor outbreak. At home we're talking epidemic!'

DICK: Oh, very funny. What about this statement – this is a country that's rife with xenophobia and anti-intellectualism? Like that bit too did you? ~~fear of people from other places.~~

MARGE: No. But the media force them to give an opinion.

DICK: No. No. Look if she has any intelligence, any common sense, she makes it abundantly clear to her interviewer that her perceptions about a place, [that she hasn't lived in for ten years], are obviously going to be outdated. And all that stuff about the father.

MARGE: But she's right! There's a whole generation of old boys like that.

DICK: Yeah, there is. But they do not represent 'the spirit of Australian life' or whatever she said. Not any more. That's the whole point. The woman's out of touch.

[*Pause*]

OK if I ring Kelly at the office?

MARGE: Why?

DICK: I think I'll get her to track down this Moynihan woman in London. I've got an idea for a piece on Australia's image problem abroad. This could fit in very nicely.

SCENE SEVENTEEN

The kitchen. TROY *is doing homework on the kitchen table.* PIP *is perusing a newspaper.* HIL *is ironing.* WAL *comes in searching for his lost glasses.*

WAL: Can't find those bloody glasses anywhere. Aw. . . What's the use of the damn things. Can't see to find 'em and when I got 'em I can read a bloody thing anyway.

HIL: Dad! You'll have to go and get yourself another prescription. This is stupid.

WAL: Yeah, yeah, yeah. . .

TROY: You'll have to get those real thick milk bottles.

WAL: [*chuckling*] I knew a bloke once, used to drink with 'im down the Koonya. His Missus used to call him MILK BOTTLE. She reckons he was always full on the front porch in the morning. [PIP *and* TROY *laugh.* HIL *rolls her eyes good humouredly.*]

HILARY: That's as old as the hills.

WAL: Still funny. Gotta admit! Troy! Come here for a sec will ya? Out here. [*He goes out onto the verandah.* TROY *follows him out.* PIP *shakes her head.*]

PIP: You know, sometimes I have to pinch myself. Just every now and again. . . I see you and I think. . . It's Mum standing there.

HIL: Yeah, ordinary and sensible. Thanks. Thanks a lot.

PIP: Oh. . . don't be offended. It's nice. It's kind of comforting. [HILARY *makes a face.* WAL *and* TROY *stand out on the balcony.*]

WAL: Listen, I been thinkin'. How 'bout you and me have a go at that book o' Meg's.

TROY: How d'you mean?

WAL: Well. . .I thought you could read it out to me. . . you know. . . just a few chapters at a time. I'm blowed if I can read m'self these days, 'less it's in bloody great big print. What d'ya reckon? Would you do that for us? [TROY *mulls this thoughtfully.*]

TROY: Yeah. OK, OK.

WAL: Good on yer. Hey Troy. . .[*He winks*] Just between the two of us, eh? She'll harp at me about goin' up to that eye bloke in Frankston. [TROY *looks reproving.*] Aw. . .Can't stand the little bastard. [WAL *leaves*] Milk bottle. Hah! Still funny!

PIP: Hil?

HIL: Mmm?

PIP: Troy asked me a few things the other day. . . about Meg's book.

> [*Pause*]

He asked me if it was about. . . his father.

> [HIL *becomes terse.*]

HIL: What gave him that idea?

PIP: I dunno.

HIL: What did you say?

> [*Pause*]

PIP: I told him it was sort of about all of us.

HIL: Why did you say that? Why did you say that, Pip?

PIP: Because he asked me straight out and I wasn't going to lie to him.

> [TROY *stands in the doorway.*]

HIL: Lie? Oh, god Pip. What is the poor kid. . . Oh, Jesus. You told a sixteen-year-old boy that some character in a book is his father. His father who he can't even remember. He was only six years old. What gave you the right to say that?

PIP: He needs to talk about it Hilary.

HIL: Oh, I'm sure he does. I'm sure he needs to talk about it now that you've thrown that into the works.

PIP: Hil. . .

HIL: What is there to talk about, hmm? Didn't anyone ever tell you about fiction? You know, make believe. . . Did you get confused somewhere. . . because it was written by your own sister? Or are you angry about something because you may have seen a bit of yourself in it that you don't particularly

like. Because if that's the case, I'm sorry. But don't put that
on me. And don't put it on my son.
WAL: [*off*] Who left their bicycle leaning against the bloody
garage door?
TROY: Coming Pop.

SCENE EIGHTEEN

The London flat.

MEG: You know, I keep wondering what Dad would make of all
of this business – the London press having a field day with
the book and me being grilled about my upbringing, my
family life and everything. I reckon he'd say 'Meggy, there
are two things you oughta know about the Poms. The first is
that they're not real keen on gettin' wet and second, they're
whingeing bastards. So all this hoo hah about your book. I
wouldn't take a jot o' notice. Just sour grapes.'
EDWIN: A genuine Antipodean Socrates, your Dad.
MEG: [*smiling*] It's all so simple. His whole way of looking at
things. . .
EDWIN: Mmm. Xenophobia and prejudice usually are.
MEG: Oh, don't be such a stuffed shirt. You'd like him. If you
met him. Everybody does.
EDWIN: Mm.
    [*Pause*]
MEG: I wish you could meet him.
EDWIN: Mmm. [*He begins to peruse the paper. He becomes
aware of* MEG *looking at him.*] I will. I'll get to meet him.
[MEG *begins to look sullen.*] Don't start. Please.
    [*Long pause*]
I must say I'm not so keen on this last bit. 'Moynihan
cannot foresee that she would ever return to Australia to
live. "I am married to an Englishman," she says, "who is
terrified of flying, could not swim to save his life, and has

a morbid fear of mosquitos and sunburn." Is that what you said?

MEG: Mm hmm. It's the only thing he got right.

SCENE NINETEEN

MARGE *is painting at her easel in the garden. She has a still life set up on a table, some fruit and a glass vase etc.* DICK *comes out.*

DICK: There goes that bright idea. Our Ms Moynihan is not available for comment apparently. Shit. Shit. Shit.

MARGE: She's a novelist remember, not a political commentator.

DICK: Well then, she should stick to discussing literature.

MARGE: Why are you so defensive, Dick? I think that's the more interesting question myself.

DICK: Defensive! It's not a personal issue, Marge.

MARGE: Isn't it?

DICK: What are you getting at?

MARGE: I'm wondering why you're so resentful?

DICK: All right. OK, I am 'resentful' if that's the word you want to use, that this kind of shit [*He waves the newspaper clipping in front of her.*] is perpetuating – on a global scale – the impression that we are still a colonial outpost. That is the source of my resentment.

MARGE: I understand that. I think, maybe, there might be something else in there, that's all.

DICK: Like what?

[*Pause*]

Marge?

MARGE: Well, it seems to me that your own work doesn't get the attention that you'd like it to. That it deserves.

DICK: So your little theory is that I'm envious. Is that it? Because I haven't 'made it' like Ms Moynihan?

MARGE: No.

DICK: Good. I'm glad of that, because I think I'm well enough read in social theory to understand that anyone who adopts a radical position is not going to have currency in the mainstream. I think I've come to terms with that. I don't think my essays are going to be published in extract form in *The Womens' Weekly*, if that's what you're suggesting. I have accepted this.

MARGE: Yes, I'm aware of that Dick.

DICK: Good. And be aware of another thing that makes me feel 'resentful'. People like her – they piss off as soon as they can, their ignorance about their own country is breathtaking and they have no qualms whatsoever about dumping on it and yet. . . in her case, the fact that she grew up in this country is at the very heart of that novel. It's the life source. Now doesn't that strike you as hypocrisy?

MARGE: I hear what you're saying.

DICK: Don't 'hear what I'm saying'. I can't stand that shit.

MARGE: OK, I don't hear what you're saying. Why should I? Stupid me! It's not as if you ever bother to actually *hear* what I'm saying or anyone else for that matter.

DICK: Oh, for god's sake Marge. It's just the language – that crappy psychological jargon. I can't stand it.

MARGE: Funny about that. I'm getting pretty sick of your crappy sociological jargon. But in this instance – it's not just the language I can't stand. It's the fact that you don't have any *other* language. [*He picks up an apple distractedly from* MARGE's 'arrangement' *and bites into it.*]

MARGE: Dick!!!!

SCENE TWENTY

London flat. It is late at night. MEG *is getting ready for bed.* EDWIN *comes in sleepily in his pyjamas. He collapses into an armchair.*

EDWIN: I'm exhausted.

MEG: Me too.

EDWIN: It's such a terrible drag having to visit one's parents isn't it? I quite like Brighton otherwise. I mean I like the seaside.

MEG: Seaside. You're so quaint sometimes. Still, you could hardly call it the beach could you?

EDWIN: We have been known to use poetic licence on occasions.

[MEG *laughs. She looks over at* EDWIN *with affection.*]

MEG: I love you.

EDWIN: Nah, it's just lust. It's these pyjamas. They have that effect on women.

[MEG *laughs*]

MEG: You know, after today I was thinking. . .

EDWIN: I know. You're never going to come to a family dinner in Brighton again. I don't blame you. I wish I could decide that.

MEG: Oh, come on. You love those dinners. Everyone yelling at each other. You're in your element.

EDWIN: Yes, I suppose I do quite like that part.

MEG: Of course you do. You've got the loudest voice. I was looking at you all this afternoon. It's like being at an exhibition of oil paintings. All hanging on separate walls, screaming at one another. But when I'm there, I always feel like this pale little watercolour hanging behind a cupboard.

[EDWIN *roars laughing.*]

I do. I think it must be your father. He has this effect on me.

[*Long pause*]

He's so hell bent on being certain about everything isn't he? I suppose most men are. It's probably the one true emblem of masculinity. The central ideal to which every man aspires: to be certain about his ideas, his actions and his place in the world.

EDWIN: What's wrong with that?

MEG: What's wrong with it is if you're preoccupied with a need to be certain, you don't allow yourself to see the

contradictions in things. And when you don't see
contradictions, your perceptions are totally blunted. I'm not
the least bit interested in being certain about anything.

EDWIN: So I've noticed.

MEG: Ah! Listen, your family always have to take up a
position. If you proffer the slightest whisper of an idea it gets
pounced upon and moulded into something unbelievably
weighty. And before you know it, you find yourself
desperately committed to something and you spend the rest
of the night under siege.

EDWIN: You're just apolitical and making excuses for it.

MEG: No I'm not. I'm just trying to understand why I feel so
odd every time I go to Brighton.

EDWIN: The pale little watercolour. I must say I've never
thought of you as that.

[MEG *smiles.*]

MEG: I miss it you know. Being part of a family.

EDWIN: Look, believe me. They think you're the best thing since
sliced bread. As far as they're concerned, you're absolutely
one of the family.

MEG: I mean my own family.

EDWIN: Oh, well. . . that's different isn't it?

[*Pause*]

MEG: I was thinking that I might go home. Just for a bit. It's
what I need. I realised after today. . . I actually need to go
home.

EDWIN: I know.

MEG: But I can't go without you, Edwin.

EDWIN: Oh.

MEG: Is that pathetic?

EDWIN: Really pathetic.

MEG: Please come with me. Just this one time. Please?

SCENE TWENTY-ONE

HILARY *and* PIP *come home late at night.* HILARY *comes into the sitting room to discover* WAL *asleep on a chair.* TROY *has crashed out on a cushion on the floor.* TROY *has a copy of* MEG's *book open on his chest. They are positioned in such a way that we may assume* TROY *has been reading to his grandfather.*

PIP: Oh, my god. Look at this.

WAL: Ah. . . must have nodded off.

    [TROY *sleeps on soundly.* PIP *comes in.*]

HIL: What's he doing here?

    [WAL *grins*]

WAL: Sleepin' by the looks of things.

HIL: Oh, Dad. . .

    [WAL *leans down and surreptitiously slips the book under his seat.*]

WAL: Well. . . d'you paint the town red.

PIP: Yeah, sure Dad. This place's really jumping.

    [*He chuckles*]

WAL: What time are you off tomorrow?

HIL: I'm driving her up to the train at half past one.

WAL: Ah hah. What are you doin' up there any rate?

    [PIP *sits down on the arm of his chair. She strokes his hair lovingly.*]

PIP: Do you know that's the first time you've asked me anything at all about what I'm doing here. Do you realise that you haven't asked me one thing about my work since I've been here?

WAL: Yeah, orright. Well I'm askin' you now aren't I?

HIL: Come on, let's get to bed. It's late. I've got to go to work in the morning.

WAL: Hang about. Got something to tell you. Come on Pippy.

    [HILARY *leans against the chair.*]

PIP : Well. . . I've landed this big account. . .

WAL: Yeah.

PIP: The agency I work for in New York's got this client and
they want to start marketing their product in Australia. So
they've sent me over here to liaise with their Australian
office, so that we can come up with a concept.

WAL: What's the product?

[PIP *grins*]

PIP: Margarine.

[WAL *roars with laughter.* TROY *wakes.*]

WAL: Trust the bloody Septics, eh? Floggin' Yank margarine to
the Aussies. An' I s'ppose you've got to come up with
something that cons us poor suckers into thinkin' this is the
real McCoy. Dinky di Aussie margarine we're buying here.

PIP: Yep. Got it in one.

WAL: Aw. . . make your socks rot wouldn't it?

HIL: Come on Troyby. Bed.

TROY: [*sleepily*] Did he tell you about Meg?

HIL: No.

[*They turn to* WAL *who is grinning smugly.*]

WAL: You better sit down for this.

[HIL *sighs, looks at her watch and plonks herself on the
arm of the couch.*]

HIL: Come on. Spit it out.

[WAL *and* TROY *exchange looks. Being the purveyors of
exciting news they want to spin it out.* WAL *indicates for*
TROY *to tell.*]

TROY: She's arriving next week.

PIP: What? Here?

TROY: Yep.

[*The two women greet this news in astonished silence.*]

PIP: Jesus.

[*Pause*]

 How come?

WAL: Well, she's missin' out, isn't she? Us all bein' here. And
she knows it. Not a real family. Without everyone.

[WAL'*s eyes begin to smart with the sentiment.*]

HIL: Oh, Dad.

[HIL *goes over and hugs him.*]

WAL: Not before time eh? [*To* PIP] And you took your time too.

[*Pause*]

PIP: Is Edwin coming?

WAL: Yeah. She's finally convinced him. That's what's been holdin' her back you know.

[HILARY *laughs.*]

HIL: Oh, Dad!

WAL: True. Silly whacker.

TROY: You don't even know him.

WAL: Hmm. I know enough.

TROY: Rubbish. It's just that he's a Pom. Isn't it?

WAL: Got nothin' to do with it.

TROY: That's bullshit Pop.

[HILARY *notices* PIP *leaving the room.*]

HIL: Pip?

TROY: Pip?

[TROY *gets up to follow her.* HILARY *holds up her hand.*]

HIL: Hang on Troy.

WAL: What's goin' on? I thought she'd be as pleased as punch.

[HILARY *shrugs*]

HIL: I'm going to bed.

[*Silence.* WAL *sighs*]

WAL: Let's hit the sack eh? Come on. [*Troy says nothing.*] Thought we might take off down the back beach in the morning. Get in a swim before breakfast. What d'ya reckon? Bring your board? [TROY *nods, distractedly.*]

TROY: OK.

SCENE TWENTY-TWO

MARGE *and* DICK *sit at a table of a small coffee shop/gourmet food deli. This is* HILARY'S *shop. She comes out to take their order.*

HILARY: Hello. How are you?

MARGE: Good thanks.

HILARY: [*to* DICK] Hi. What can I get you?

DICK: Hi. Just two cappuccinos please.

HILARY: Okey doke.

> [HIL *goes behind the counter.*]

MARGE: Er. . . excuse me, I hope you don't think this is presumptuous, but er. . . I was wondering. . . whether you were Hilary Moynihan.

HILARY: Yes, I am. Well I was.

MARGE: Related to Meg Moynihan?

> [HILARY *laughs.*]

HILARY: Yep. She's my sister.

MARGE: Uh. Well I just wanted to say. . . er. . . I am sorry, my name's Marge Morrissey. . . I have a holiday house down on the Back Beach road. And this is a friend of mine, Dick Bennett.

HILARY: Hi.

MARGE: I'd just like to say that. . . I loved your sister's book. I think. . . it's one of the most beautiful books I've ever read. And I. . . just wanted to tell you. That's all.

> [HILARY *smiles warmly at* MARGE.]

HILARY: Thank you. Well, thank you on her behalf. She'd be very touched by that. I'll tell her.

MARGE: Would you?

HILARY: Sure. She'll be here next week as a matter of fact.

MARGE: Oh.

DICK: Sorrento?

HILARY: Yeah. Oh, you're not from the press I hope?

DICK: No.

> [*Pause*]

MARGE: No.

HILARY: Oh, good. It's supposed to be a secret. She doesn't want the place crawling with journalists apparently.

> [HILARY *laughs and shakes her head a little disbelievingly.*]

DICK: No. Good idea.

MARGE: She's coming home to her family.

HILARY: Yeah. Next Wednesday.

MARGE: How lovely.

HILARY: We haven't seen her since. . . well I met her in Italy in. . .'85. . . so that's six years ago. But she hasn't been home for . . .years.

MARGE: Oh, that'll be wonderful. A lovely family re-union.

HIL: Yeah.

MARGE: We won't tell anybody. Will we?

DICK: Er. . . no. We certainly won't.

[HILARY *laughs. The phone rings.*]

HILARY: Ah! Excuse me. Won't be a moment.

[HILARY *leaves*]

DICK: You bloody beauty. This is my lucky day. You little bloody beauty. The woman is going to be in town and no-one else from the media knows. [*He looks skywards.*]

MARGE: You are not from the press remember?

DICK: We'll work something out.

MARGE: Don't you dare. I mean it Dick. People are entitled to their privacy. . .

[HILARY *suddenly bursts into the room.*]

HILARY: Oh, my god.

[*She stands in the room in a state of near hysteria and panic, looking around her frantically, moving from one spot to another, looking for keys, anything.*]

Oh, no. Oh, no. I'm sorry. I'm sorry. Oh, no. I have to go. Oh, god. I'm sorry.

MARGE: What dear? What?

[*She stands staring at* MARGE *in a state of utter panic.*]

HILARY: My father. He's gone missing. In the sea.

[*Blackout*]

END OF ACT ONE

ACT TWO

SCENE ONE

The three sisters are sitting at the end of the jetty. Over to their right, EDWIN *is paddling in the shallows. The atmosphere is infused with a sense of melancholy.*

HILARY: Do you remember the Sorrento fair? [*Both* PIP *and* MEG *nod in recollection.*] Remember the year the fortune teller came?

MEG: He wasn't a fortune teller, was he?

HIL: What was he then?

PIP: He was a 'world renowned' palmist and clairvoyant. Punditt Maharaji.

MEG: That's right. It was written on the caravan. Punditt Maharaji.

HIL: What did he tell you? Do you remember?

MEG: Not really. Something like 'You are going to be rich and famous and travel vast distances across the sea.'
     [*They smile.*]

HIL: What about you Pip?

PIP: Er. . . rich and famous and travel vast distances. Something highly personalised like that.

HIL: Do you know what he said to me? He said I was one of three.

PIP: That was a good guess.

MEG: What else?

HIL: That was it. The Rixon kids threw stones at the caravan and he went off after them.

PIP: I don't think you got your shilling's worth.

[*They muse over the memory. In the distance* PIP *sees* TROY *walking alone at the top of the cliff. He is looking out to sea.*]

PIP: There's Troy.

[*The other women look in that direction. They watch silently. There is a change in mood.*]

Still looking for Pop.

[*Silence*]

MEG: Poor kid. The sea will never give up its dead.

HIL: He's a different boy isn't he? He's just clammed up. He loved Dad so much. They had something very special those two. It's not fair is it?

[*Silence*]

People are always dying on him.

PIP: He's a survivor Hil. He is.

HIL: Yeah. . . but at what cost?

[*Pause.* MEG *looks at her penetratingly.* HIL *looks away.*]

PIP: What do you mean?

HIL: He feels responsible this time.

[*Silence*]

MEG: Yes. I know what that's like. [*They stare out to sea.* MEG *waits for a response. None is forthcoming.*] I think I'll go for a walk. [PIP *and* HILARY *say nothing.* MEG *makes her way over to* EDWIN.]

PIP: She can't concede can she, that anyone else could be hurting as much as she is? She's like a child.

[*Silence*]

You think I'm still an angry young thing, don't you? You may think this is bullshit, but I'm different when I'm away. I'm a different person. If you met any of my friends in New York and you said, 'Pippa's such a cot case isn't she?' they wouldn't know what you were talking about.

HILARY: I don't think you're a cot case.

PIPPA: Oh, I am. I know I am. But only when I'm here.

HILARY: Must be in the water.

PIPPA: I really did want people to see how much I'd changed. I was really looking forward to coming home you know. But people don't want to see that do they? They don't want to see what's new about you. They're suspicious of that. It's like you've reneged on who you are. And that's fixed. That's immutable. You are who you are and if you try and change, you must be faking. Bunging on an act. But over there people think differently. In fact, if you're not working to make positive changes in your life, they think you're in deep shit.

HIL: Yeah. So I hear.

PIP: You're cynical about that, aren't you?

HIL: No. I'm just not so sure that people actually *do* change.

PIP: Everybody has the potential. It's just whether we choose to take up on it or not.

HIL: Sounds like propaganda to me. I think I'd rather be saying, 'OK, this is who I am. Like it or lump it. May as well get used to it, and make the best of it'.

[PIPPA *makes no response. She looks out to sea.*]

SCENE TWO

In the shallows.

EDWIN: What's up?

[MEG *sighs*]

MEG: 'We shall not cease from exploration.
  And the end of all our exploring
  will be to arrive at where we started
  and know the place for the first time.'

EDWIN: T.S. Elliot.

MEG: Mm. I had hoped that I would know the place for the first time. But I'm not sure that I know it any better than when I left.

EDWIN: Things change in ten years Meg.

MEG: No. They haven't. That's just it. It's like there's this highly elasticised thread that's tied around us three and it stretches from Australia to Britain and to the States and all of a sudden it's just given out and thwack we're flung back together again. And we're just the same little girls, but this time in women's bodies. And we don't know any more than when we started out. [*Sighing*] I'm beginning to feel quite middle aged.

EDWIN: I'm not surprised. This town feels like everyone in it was born into middle age. D'you know, the only conversations I've had since we arrived, have been about children and compost.

MEG: People don't know what to say to us. Grief makes people realise how inadequate they are.

EDWIN: Yes.

   [*Pause*]

Tell me, does anything ever happen here?

MEG: No. People live out quiet prosaic ineffectual lives and then they die. And the other people spend the rest of their lives utterly emotionally crippled by the experience. That seems to be the pattern.

   [*Silence*]

EDWIN: I must say, Hilary is quite a remarkable woman isn't she?

MEG: Why do you say that?

EDWIN: The way she copes with things.

MEG: Oh, yes. Hilary copes. She 'copes' because she shuts down. That's the way she lives her life. She doesn't let herself feel. She doesn't think about things too deeply. It's like she made a decision a long time ago that she was done with crying. Nothing or nobody was ever going to hurt her again. So she 'copes' magnificently and people think she's so strong, so remarkable. I don't. I think she's a coward.

   [*Silence*]

EDWIN: I think you're being very unfair. I can't imagine what it must be like for her. She's had to deal with three deaths. All of them tragic. I can't even begin to think how one would ever really deal with that.

MEG: No, perhaps you can't.

EDWIN: And I don't think you can either.

MEG: They were my parents too, Edwin. . .

EDWIN: I know.

MEG: And I was here, remember, when Gary died.

EDWIN: I know. But he wasn't your husband Meg.

MEG: No, he wasn't my husband. But I loved him. That's what you don't understand. I loved him too.

SCENE THREE

HILARY and PIP *make their way up the path to the house. They stop for a breather and take in the view.*

HILARY: I dreamt last night that I married Edwin.

PIP: Whoa, that was nasty.

HILARY: I forgot to shave my legs.

PIP: Oh, Hil. That was an oversight.

HILARY: I know. I was wearing a short white dress and these terrible hairy legs. I just couldn't enjoy myself.

PIP: I can imagine. Did he wear pyjamas?

HILARY: No. He was wearing a purple suit.

[PIPPA *bursts out laughing.*]

PIP: I mean afterwards, you dill.

HIL: I didn't get that far. I woke up about half way through the reception.

PIP: That was lucky. You know I can't get my head around the possibility that anyone could actually lust after Eddie.

[HIL *laughs despite herself.*]

HIL: Oh, Pippa. You're dreadful. He's not that bad.

PIP: He is. He's ridiculous. Look at him down there. 'Paddling'. God help us. Anyway, I've always found Englishmen rather ridiculous. Well, can you imagine it. Grown men referring to their penises as their 'willies'. It's very off putting.

[*The two women walk up the path to the verandah.* TROY *comes out of the house.*]

HIL: Troy?

TROY: Yeah.

HIL: Who was that, driving off?

TROY: That guy Dick Bennett.

HIL: What did he want?

[TROY *holds up a single rose in a cellophane cylinder.*]

TROY: He left this.

HIL: He must be down for the weekend.

PIP: Who?

HIL: The guy who drove me to the beach . . .that day.

TROY: I think he's got the hots for you.

HIL: Don't be silly Troy. [HILARY *takes the rose and reads the card.*] What makes you say that?

TROY: He asked me if I wanted to go fishing.

PIP: Uh huh? That makes sense. A way to a woman's heart is a bucket of fresh flathead.

TROY: You'd be surprised the number of boring old farts that come round here with flowers asking me to go fishing.

HIL: Oh sure, Troy. They're bashing down the doors.

PIP: Maybe they've got the hots for you. Nice young boy like you. Anything's possible.

[TROY *gives her a 'don't be smart' look.*]

HIL: What did you say anyway?

TROY: 'No', of course. I don't want to go fishing with him.

[*He gets up to leave.*]

HIL: Why don't you go over and see one of your mates?

[TROY *shrugs and goes indoors.* HIL *and* PIP *exchange looks.* HILARY *sighs.*]

PIP: What's the card say?

HILARY: With deepest sympathy.

[PIP *nods*]

PIP: Do they really come round here asking him to go fishing.

HIL: What do you reckon?

[*Silence*]

PIP: You know what I reckon. I reckon you ought to pack up
and leave.

[HIL *stops in her tracks.*]

You're marking time Hil. You've been marking time for
years. Now's your chance.

SCENE FOUR

MEG *is wandering alone through the cemetery. A light rain is
beginning to fall.* TROY *hovers some distance away, unseen by*
meg.

TROY: Meg? Aunt Meg?

[MEG *looks up and smiles wanly.* TROY *approaches
gingerly. He hands her a coat.*]

Thought you might need this.

MEG: Thank you.

[*They stand together silently for a while.*]

I used to come here when I was a kid. Just wander around
and read the tombstones. I still remember the names.
Charlotte Grace Phelps and Frederic Earnest Phelps. See,
September 12, 1890 and October 1, 1890. He died three
weeks later. Lottie and Fred. D'you think he died of a
broken heart? I used to imagine that he found life
intolerable without her. Can you imagine loving someone so
much that you just couldn't go on?

[*Pause*]

[TROY *shrugs*]

TROY: I just wanted to say that we read your book, Pop and
me, but. . . we didn't finish it.

[MEG *nods*]

MEG: It's only a book.

TROY: He asked me to read it to him. We used to read it on the
verandah when Mum was at work. We only had two chapters
to go. [*He sighs*] I tried to read them last night. . .but. . . [*He
shakes his head.*]

[*Pause*]
D'you know the part I liked best?
MEG: No?
TROY: When Helen and Grace meet in Italy.
MEG: That's the thing you have to be careful about with fiction.
It leads us to believe that reconciliations are possible.
TROY: What d'you mean?

[TROY *looks at her intently, obviously wanting a response.*]

MEG: People coming together. . . reconciling their differences.
It doesn't always happen.
TROY: It doesn't happen in real life, you mean?
MEG: Not always. No.
TROY: Well, why did you write it then?

[MEG *makes no reply.*]

SCENE FIVE

EDWIN *stands on the balcony of the verandah looking out to sea.*
PIP *is sitting on the steps.* HIL *comes out. They both look down at* MEG *walking alone along the beach.*

EDWIN: 'Lost Angel of a ruin'd Paradise!
She knew not t'was her own; as with no stain
She faded like a cloud which had outwept its rain.'

[HIL *and* PIP *exchange looks.*]

EDWIN: Shelley.
HILARY: Ah. [*Long pause.*] I thought you might like a beer.
EDWIN: Yes. Thank you. That'd be nice.

[HILARY *hands him a can. He expects a glass, but as none is forthcoming, he pulls the ring off the top of the can and sips tentatively.*]

It's really very beautiful isn't it. It grows on you I think.
HIL: Mm.
EDWIN: Poor Meg. She looks so fragile doesn't she?

[PIPPA *rolls her eyes, unseen by* EDWIN.]

Well, I don't suppose you know where Troy is, do you?
[HIL *shrugs.*]

HILARY: I think he might be in his room.

EDWIN: I thought he and I might go fishing tomorrow.
[PIPPA *bursts out laughing.* HIL *suppresses a grin.* EDWIN
looks vaguely hurt.]

PIPPA: Sorry, Eddie. Bit of a private joke.
[EDWIN *manages a weak grin. He goes to leave, then
turns to* PIPPA.]

EDWIN: By the way, if you could manage it. . . I'd really rather
be called Edwin.

PIPPA: OK, Edwin it is.

EDWIN: Thanks.
[*Once out of earshot*]

PIPPA: No wuz, Eddie ol' bean! [HIL *gives her a withering look.*]
Shelley.

HIL: Pip.

PIP: She looks so fragile.

HIL: Don't be a bitch.

PIP: I'm not. It just turns my stomach that's all.

HIL: He loves her. God! I'd give my eye teeth for someone to
love me like that. Wouldn't you?

SCENE SIX

MARGE *and* DICK *are sitting on the verandah of* MARGE'*s
holiday house.*

MARGE: I saw her on the jetty today. She's quite plump really.
That's odd isn't it?

DICK: What?

MARGE: Well, her being a rather large, big boned sort of
woman.

DICK: What's odd about that?

MARGE: I don't know. I suppose I expected her to be fragile.
You know, rather slight with fine bones and long fingers.

[MARGE *smiles, not without irony. Pause*]

DICK: I thought I might wander over there this afternoon.

[MARGE *looks at him sideways.*]

MARGE: Oh.

DICK: Yeah, just to see how they're getting on.

MARGE: Hilary, you mean.

[DICK *shrugs. Pause*]

Were you wanting to see Hilary?. . . Or Meg?

DICK: Well, Hilary I suppose. I haven't met 'Ms' Moynihan.

MARGE: Don't you think that's a bit intrusive.

[*Pause*]

DICK: Well we got a bit involved.

[*Pause*]

MARGE: Don't use that please.

DICK: What do you mean?

MARGE: I'd just hate to think that you'd use the situation to get your interview with Meg. That's all.

DICK: What do you think I am?

MARGE: A journalist.

[*The muscle in his jaw is twitching.*]

DICK: Ah. Well that's very telling isn't it? → keeping it inside

[DICK*'s anger is imploding. He stands. He leans on the balcony. He doesn't know what to do with himself.*]

MARGE: I'm sorry if I've. . . hurt your feelings.

DICK: Oh, don't worry about it Marge. I don't have any feelings. Remember? I'm a journalist. We're the lowest of the low. I'm just sorry I didn't have my camera with me. I could have got some really good snaps. I mean I was first on the scene, remember? I could have got the sister and the nephew. The whole damn page one horror story.

SCENE SEVEN

MEG *comes into the kitchen where* PIP *and* HIL *are sitting.*

PIP: Meg, we were just talking about the estate. We have to make an appointment with the solicitor. You free tomorrow?

MEG: He didn't have any money to speak of, did he?

HIL: Not much. But there's. . . the house. We have to decide what to do about it.

MEG: What d'you mean?

PIPPA: Whether to sell it or not.

MEG: Sell it? You can't be serious?

> [*Pause. She looks from one to the other and fixes on* HILARY.]

It's your home. Why would we want to sell it?

HILARY: It belongs to the three of us now.

MEG: So what? You live here. I mean that's fine by me. Isn't that fine by you Pip?

PIP: She's thinking of moving up to Melbourne. Which I think's a very good idea.

MEG: [*To* HILARY] You didn't tell me this.

HILARY: I haven't made up my mind. . . yet. And I'm only one of three. I suppose I wondered how you felt about it.

MEG: I feel terrible.

PIP: Why? You don't live here. You haven't lived here for ten years. And the way I see it, is that Hilary has been the one to look after Dad for all these years while you and I have been able to do exactly as we please. So I think it's up to her to say what she wants.

MEG: And what do you want, Pip?

PIPPA: I want what Hilary wants. And since she's the one who's made the sacrifice. . .

MEG: Please don't tell me about Hilary's sacrifice. She is the one who made the choice. Hilary. You made the choice.

PIPPA: There was no other choice.

MEG: She made the choice.

PIPPA: What was the choice? That we had a nurse for the two years after he had the heart attack. Got in a housekeeper. Meals on wheels. Don't be ridiculous Meg. There was no choice. Were *you* prepared to come back here and look after him?

HILARY: Pippa, please.

MEG: No. I was not prepared to come back here. You know that. But other arrangements could have been made.

PIPPA: Like what?

MEG: I don't know because it didn't come to that.

PIPPA: Because Hilary said she'd step in.

MEG: Yes. She made a choice.

[PIPPA *is fuming.*]

HILARY: It's OK, Pip.

PIPPA: No it's not OK. I think we owe you something. I think we owe you a great deal. And I'm sorry that Meg doesn't feel like that. In fact I think it's disgusting.

MEG: Well you're a child.

PIPPA: Is that all you can say?

MEG: It's our home. Our family home.

PIPPA: Not any more.

HILARY: It is Pip.

PIP: It's not. You live in England for godsake. It's not your home.

MEG: And you're doing your best to make me feel like that.

PIPPA: Jesus Christ.

SCENE EIGHT

EDWIN *and* TROY *are fishing off the jetty*

TROY: Did you ever meet my Dad?

EDWIN: No. I met Meg after she came to London.

TROY: Oh, yeah, that's right.

[*Silence*]

TROY: How come she went. Do you know?

EDWIN: Well, I suppose she wanted to travel. Most Aussie's have the travel bug don't they?

TROY: Yeah. Pop used to say that he couldn't understand why people wanted to do it. 'Why would anyone want to leave a place like this?' He was always saying that.

EDWIN: Perhaps he had a point.

TROY: He said people only travelled when they needed to run away.

[*Pause*]

EDWIN: Well two of his daughters did travel. What did he say about that?

TROY: He said they were running away.

EDWIN: Oh, I don't really believe that. Do you?

[TROY *shrugs.*]

TROY: I don't know what to believe. I don't think there's much use staying put. Just for the sake of it.

[*Pause*]

There's nothing much to do here. Not any more.

SCENE NINE

HILARY *sits alone on the beach.* MARGE *approaches.*

MARGE: Hilary?

HILARY: Oh, hello. How are you?

MARGE: I'm OK. How are you - more to the point?

HILARY: Oh. . . bearing up. By the way - I've been meaning to write you a note - I'm sorry I just haven't got around to it.

MARGE: Of course you haven't. Don't be silly.

HILARY: I wanted to thank you for all your help. That day and everything. You and Dick.

MARGE: I just feel so sorry. I can't stop thinking about you all.

HILARY: Yeah.

[*Pause*]

Do you want to sit down?

MARGE: You don't want to be on your own?

HILARY: No. I think I'll go potty if I spend too much time on my own. So, how's it going at your place?

MARGE: Oh, pretty good. Dick's down again this week.

HILARY: Yeah.

MARGE: He's been coming down quite a bit lately. Driving me nuts.

[*She laughs.* HIL *smiles.*]

HILARY: I thought you two were the best of mates.

MARGE: Oh, yes we are I suppose. He's just been getting on my quince a bit lately.

HILARY: Really?

MARGE: I can't be bothered with men much these days! Terrible thing to say isn't it? But I'm afraid it's the truth.

[HIL *laughs*]

He's such an ideologue. It's a bit like having lunch with a text book.

HILARY: Is he a teacher too?

MARGE: No. Used to be, but no, now he's a writer. He writes political stuff, cultural analysis, that sort of thing.

HILARY: I think I'd be out of my depth there.

MARGE: No, not necessarily. Anyway he's totally out of his depth when it comes to relating to women. Anyone probably. I used to find him quite intimidating you know, because he seemed so clever and articulate. But now. . .[*She scoffs*]

HILARY: You should be at the dinner table at our place. With Meg and her husband. I'm sure they must think I'm a complete dummy.

MARGE: I doubt it.

HILARY: You know, I used to think that when my sisters had children they'd have to stop for a bit. And that'd be my chance to catch up. So when they were up to their elbows in nappies and all that business, I'd be out there doing all the things that they've been able to do. But it doesn't work like that does it?

[MARGE *smiles.*]

They'd be able to have their children without the slightest hiccough, those two girls.

MARGE: Hard to say. They might be totally bamboozled by it.

HILARY: I doubt it. They're so competent in every other way - motherhood isn't that hard.

MARGE: Millions'd disagree of course.

[*Pause*]

You sound like Helen.

HILARY: Who's Helen?

MARGE: Helen, in the book.

HILARY: Oh, yeah. That'd be right. The parochial one. That's me.

local one

MARGE: She's my favourite character actually.

HIL: Is she?

MARGE: Oh, yes. [MARGE *smiles*.]

[*Pause*]

I was so much like Helen. . .

[MARGE *pauses, lost in thought. She glances at* HILARY *who looks at her questioningly*.]

. . .except that I don't think I was betrayed quite so terribly as she was. My husband left me for another woman when the children were little. Oh, years and years ago now. And I behaved just like Helen — so 'adult' about it all. Well I had to be I suppose. I was always seeing them because we were constantly ferrying the children back and forth between the two households.

[*Pause.*]

I was so nice to them, you know. I had such little self esteem that I was able to completely understand or at least rationalise why he'd want to team up with her. She was everything I wasn't. And because I wanted the children to be able to cope with the divorce and the split households, I kind of promoted them as a couple. I told the children they were lucky to have her. She'd be able to show them and tell them things about the world that I couldn't. I gave her such good publicity. . . and it worked. And I paid for it. Not that the children lost respect for me, necessarily. . . and I think they've always loved me. . . but I don't feel as though they know me.

[Pause]

I'm not a known quantity. To my children. And I know
exactly why I did it. I couldn't bear my children to see me
being so resentful and bitter. Which is exactly how I felt.

[Pause]

So I suppose that's why I understood Helen. She couldn't
really vent her spleen ever, could she? She had too much to
lose. Or at least that's how she saw it. So, she just went on
coping. . . and everyone thought she was strong.

SCENE TEN

MEG *is in the garden,* PIPPA *comes out.*

PIPPA: Meg?
MEG: Mm?
PIPPA: I'm sorry.
    [Pause]
MEG: Pip, I've been carrying guilt for too long. I don't need you
    to lump it on me again.
    [Silence. PIPPA *looks frightened.]*
PIPPA: I haven't lumped anything on you.
MEG: Haven't you?
PIP: Look, I don't want to talk about all that.
MEG: You never want to talk about it. You never have and you
    never will.
PIP: It's in the past Meg.
MEG: You ask Troy whether he thinks it's in the past. I don't
    know what to say to him Pip. Do you know? Or do you just
    change the topic? Or perhaps he doesn't ask you about Gary,
    because he asks me.
    *[*PIP *says nothing.]*
PIPPA: What do you want me to do Meg? What do you want me
    to say? Hmm?
    *[*MEG *closes her eyes. Long pause]*
MEG: I think I hurt his feelings this morning.

PIPPA: Well you're a shit!

MEG: Oh, god Pippa. Don't you have any softness about you at all? Do you have to cut at everything.

> [PIPPA *is cut to the quick. She says nothing. Silence.* MEG *goes to touch her arm.* PIPPA *flinches.*]

PIPPA: He's only a boy remember. I don't want him to have to hurt any more than he is already. That's all.

> [*The flywire screen bangs and* TROY *comes out onto the verandah. He comes over to where the women are standing.*]

How are you ol' bean?

TROY: Mum said to say that she's asked that guy Dick Bennett and Marge someone or other, over for lunch. That OK with you guys?

PIPPA and MEG: Shit.

PIPPA: She's always been the sociable one of the family.

SCENE ELEVEN

The lunch. EDWIN *and* DICK *are on the verandah. The sounds of chatter and laughter are heard from the kitchen. It is as though they are waiting for the women to come out. There is an awkward silence. They drink from cans of beer.*

DICK: So, you're in publishing?

EDWIN: Yes. It's just a small concern really. I'm in partnership with another chap and we do about twenty books a year.

DICK: What sort of stuff?

EDWIN: Oh. . . coffee table books mostly.

> [*He laughs self-deprecatingly.*]

We do a lot of art books. Architecture, historic buildings. That sort of thing. We've done the occasional cookery book. Against my better judgement I might add.

DICK: I wouldn't have thought the English had much of a culinary tradition.

EDWIN: Ah. . . no. That's not strictly true. There's quite a resurgence of interest in it at the moment – it's highly fashionable to know about food and wine. The art of entertaining. Among certain sections of the community of course.

DICK: And I suppose they're the very same sections who are doing very nicely thank you out of the present government?

EDWIN: Yes.

DICK: I don't suppose you've ever considered grubbying your hands with anything more political?

[*At this moment* TROY *comes in.*]

EDWIN: I don't think it's a question of grubbying one's hands actually. I think it's merely a matter of expertise. Ah Troy. You know. . . er. . . Dick? Dick Bennett – Troy.

TROY: Yeah. G'day.

DICK: How's things?

TROY: OK.

EDWIN: Excuse me for a moment.

[TROY *and* DICK *remain in freeze.* EDWIN *walks to the kitchen on the premise of refilling glasses. He is intercepted by* MEG *coming through the door. He speaks in a low voice.*]

EDWIN: Who is that man?

MEG: I don't know.

EDWIN: I think I can feel a headache coming on.

MEG: Don't you dare. Edwin. You promised.

EDWIN: I did no such thing.

[MEG *joins* MARGE *in the lounge room.* PIP *talks to* HIL *in the kitchen.*]

PIP: So, that's Dick Bennett. The man of the rose. He's OK actually. Terrible name though.

HILARY: Why?

PIP: Well, it's so definitional. 'I feel very strongly about you Dick!'

[EDWIN *rejoins the men and fills their glasses.*]

EDWIN: Traditional Australian gathering by the looks of it. Men in one room, women in the other. Isn't that how it goes?
[*He grins.*]

TROY: Yeah.

EDWIN: I've never really been able to understand that you know. I mean as far as I'm concerned, I've always thought that Australian women were amongst the loveliest in the world. And yet the men - your average Aussie bloke - doesn't seem to be all that interested in them. That's always struck me as being very peculiar.

DICK: I think that's a bit of a cliché, actually.

TROY: You reckon?

EDWIN: Well I've got a bit of a theory about this. I'd be interested to hear what you think. I suspect all this mateship business is quite possibly a way of disguising a deeper stratum of misogyny in the Australian male.
[*Pause*]
What do you think Troy? [TROY *shrugs*] You see I don't find it at all surprising that the feminist voice is at its most strident in Australia. It's always struck me that this is a very male culture and as a result the struggle for women is by necessity more vehement here.

DICK: Compared to where? Britain?

EDWIN: Yes. I think so. Well, for example, in Britain, there are so many women moving into top executive positions these days.

DICK: That may be so, but your lot has just dumped a woman Prime Minister who wasn't exactly a paragon of liberal enlightenment. Look, if feminism is only about women making it – then it's a crock of shit as far as I'm concerned. What matters is what women actually do, when they have made it.
[*The two men drain their glasses.* TROY *aware of the tension finds this slightly amusing.* HILARY *and* PIP *enter carrying food.*]

HILARY: OK. Everyone. Food.

[TROY *seizes the opportunity to make a getaway.*]

TROY: Great, I'm starving.

[*Everyone assembles in the living room.* TROY *pinches a piece of bread.* PIPPA *slaps his hand.*]

PIP: Starving are you? Could you eat a horse?

TROY: Yes.

PIP: Good.

[*She lifts the lid off the casserole and* TROY *looks in. He looks dubious.*]

That's all he had. The butcher. I begged and pleaded but. .

HIL: Shut up you two. It's chicken   cacciatore. Sit anywhere you like.

MEG: This looks great Hil.

[*There is general assent.*]

MARGE: Who did this painting?

[*Referring to a painting on the wall. The family members all smile at the mention of the painting.*]

PIP: A bloke called Clarrie Evans.

HILARY: He was a local. He's dead now.

PIP: He was such a whacker. That's him on the far left.

MEG: Dad gave him a hand building a chicken coop in his backyard and Clarrie was so grateful he did this painting 'specially for him.

HILARY: Dad was so funny about it wasn't he? He wasn't real keen on the idea of having one of Clarrie's works of art, but as soon as he laid eyes on it. . . he loved that painting. It was his pride and joy wasn't it?

[*The family members all nod their assent.*]

MARGE: It's this house isn't it?

TROY: Yeah.

[MARGE *squints at the picture, reading the sign hanging from the verandah.*]

MARGE: Hotel Sorrento?

HILARY: Dad and all his mates used to sit out on the verandah and have a few beers. They called it Hotel Sorrento.

PIPPA: They're all dead now. Every one of those blokes.

[*Referring to the figures in the painting*]
Clarrie, Mick Hennessy, Jock Farrell, Grabber Carmichael.
EDWIN: Grabber?
HILARY: Best full forward Sorrento's ever had.
PIPPA: You know, when I'm away, and I'm thinking about home
   – that's the thing I remember. Those summer evenings,
   they'd all be out there, listening to the cricket. Drinking and
   laughing.
MEG: And drinking and drinking. . .
PIPPA: I was thinking about this the other day. . . If I had to say
   what my Dad taught me. . . as a kid. . .
HILARY: Never back a two-year-old in the wet.
   [*They laugh*]
PIP: Yeah.
   [*Pause*]
   I grew up believing that the penultimate sign of weakness in
   a man was when he couldn't hold his grog. The ultimate
   sign was if he ordered lemonade in a pub. That kind of man
   was highly untrustworthy. Funny isn't it?
MEG: Pathetic really. Considering they were all drunks.
PIP: Our Mum used to run around after them. Taking out trays
   of cold meat and cheese and tomatoes and stuff. There was
   never any room in the fridge. Remember? It was always full
   of bottles.
MEG: She couldn't even afford to buy herself a dress at
   Christmas.
HILARY: She wouldn't have had it any other way.
MEG: You reckon? She never had any friends of her own. It was
   all right with the blokes, because they wouldn't notice. But
   with women - I think she felt terrible.
HILARY: What do you mean?
MEG: I think she was ashamed of her house, her clothes, the
   state of the back yard. She never went out visiting and she
   certainly never invited anyone back here. I think she was
   desperately lonely.
   [*Pause*]

MARGE: And I suppose she never complained?

HILARY: Oh, no. She complained all right. Loud and clear.

PIP: She harped and whinged and nagged. All the time. And in the end it killed her.

MEG: She got cancer.

>[*Long pause*]
>
>What do you do Dick?
>
>[MARGE *and* DICK *exchange looks.*]

DICK: I write.

MEG: Oh, really? Fiction?

DICK: No.

MEG: What then?

PIPPA: Non-fiction.

>[TROY *laughs.*]

DICK: Essays.

MEG: Mmm.

EDWIN: Essays. I've always thought that was a very honourable pursuit. I like essays. I think it's one of the most delicious of the literary forms.

HILARY: Everybody got everything. Salad Marge?

MARGE: Oh, no thanks dear.

EDWIN: It comes from the French. 'Essayer' to try, to attempt. Thank you. What's your subject?

DICK: Australia. Contemporary Australia.

EDWIN: Right. Fairly vast I would have thought.

DICK: I edit a bi-monthly paper.

>[*Everyone stops and looks at* DICK.]

TROY: Which one?

DICK: *The Australian Voice.*

TROY: Oh, yeah. Pop used to buy that.

PIP: No he didn't.

TROY: He did.

HILARY: Oh, that pink paper.

DICK: That's the one.

HILARY: So you're the editor?

DICK: Yeah.

HILARY: Well then, you'd better own up Troy.

TROY: What?

HILARY: [*to* DICK] Remember that article on the motor industry. Beginning of the year. Did you write that by any chance?

DICK: No.

HILARY: Phew. That was lucky.

TROY: Mum!

HILARY: Troy got an 'A' for an essay on the motor industry.

PIPPA: Hey, good on you Troyby.

HILARY: Word for word was it Troy?

TROY: Get off. I changed it around. . . Sort of.

[*Everyone laughs*]

MEG: Fancy Dad buying it.

HILARY: Dad said it was the only paper that gave the working man credit for having a brain.

MEG: What about the working woman?

HILARY, PIP and

TROY: If you're a woman and you got any brains – you don't work!

PIP: Big champion of the feminist movement our Dad!

TROY: He was coming around.

EDWIN: 'Let us sit and mock the good housewife
Fortune from her wheel, that her gifts may
henceforth be bestowed equally.'

MEG: What are you talking about?

EDWIN: Shakespeare.

[*Pause*]

Terrific bean salad Hil.

[MEG *gives him a look.* EDWIN *grins impishly.*]

DICK: If he was down on feminism, what did he make of your book?

[*Pause*]

MEG: I don't know. I didn't have a chance to ask him.

[*Silence*]

TROY: He liked it. What he read of it.

[*Pause*]

But he said he didn't think you understood about loyalty.

[*Pause*]

MEG: Loyalty to whom?

TROY: He just said that loyalty was the most important quality a person could have.

[*Silence. No-one quite knows what to say.*]

MARGE: Do you think he would have argued that loyalty was more important than truth?

HIL: Yes. I think he would have. Loyalty was a big issue for him. Sticking by your mates. . . all of that.

[*Silence*]

EDWIN: I think people hold on to these things, like the notion of loyalty, or truth, as if they were unassailable which means that they lead fairly unexamined lives I would have thought. Er. . . with respect to your father. I was just speaking generally.

MARGE: Oh, I agree absolutely. It's like religion. It makes life so easy. Once you've signed up, you don't have to ask so many questions.

MEG: Exactly.

DICK: I suppose as a writer, this sort of thing must come up for you quite a lot.

MEG: What sort of thing?

DICK: The issue of loyalty. Writing as you do, so autobiographically. . .

[EDWIN *scoffs.*]

MEG: I don't write autobiography. I write fiction.

MARGE: There is a significant difference.

DICK: All right. Fiction. It's just that the connection with Sorrento is fairly obvious. . .

MARGE: I don't think it was *obvious*. In fact I don't think you would have made any connection, would you, unless I'd pointed it out?

[DICK *sighs. He is irritated.*]

DICK: I don't actually think that's the point Marge.

EDWIN: What is the point?

DICK: Well, just this business about loyalty. OK, you don't write autobiography as such, but to me your writing has a very personal feel and I wonder if people ever take offence.

MEG: It hasn't come up.

DICK: So it's not an issue for you?

MEG: Oh, yes, it's an issue. But it hasn't come up.

[*Pause*]

No-one's ever raised it. That's what I mean. In fact, I've been home for ten days and this is the first time the book's been mentioned.

TROY: No it's not.

MEG: Oh, yes. Sorry. You and I had a bit of a talk about it, didn't we?

[*To her sisters*]

But you two haven't said a solitary word about it. I don't even know whether you've read it.

PIP: 'Course I've read it.

MEG: [*to* HIL] Have you?

HIL: Mmm.

MEG: Well, why haven't you said anything to me?

EDWIN: Meg. Come on. That's a bit unfair.

MEG: Why is it unfair? Talk about loyalty.

PIP: There have been a few other things going on Meg.

[*Silence*]

DICK: Well I'm quite happy to talk about it.

MARGE: Dick.

[MEG *ignores* DICK *and continues to address her sisters.*]

MEG: It *has* been nominated for the Booker prize. It's not a completely insignificant piece of work. Not that you'd bloody know it round here.

[*Pause*]

You know Dick, people used to ask me why I stayed in London. Why I didn't come home. And I used to say it was because the artist has no status in this country. Why make art when you can make money? That's Australia for you.

But I'm talking ten years ago. I was sure things would have
changed. . .

MARGE: But they have. There's been significant changes. . .

MEG: Look there's all this talk about the new renaissance in
Australian culture. The literature, the cinema, the theatre.
Aboriginal art, taking the world by storm. Australian
novelists getting huge coverage in the *New York Book
Review*. All of that. But the fact is, in this country there is a
suffocatingly oppressive sense that what you do as an artist,
is essentially self indulgent.

DICK: How do you know? You've only been here for ten days
but you've been away for ten years.

MEG: I know because I lived here for thirty years. I went away.
And now I'm back. *Nothing* has changed.

DICK: See I think you're wrong. And I can't for the life of me
see how you can feel so authoritative about this. Like that
interview in *The Guardian*.

MARGE: Dick.

DICK: I'm sorry but I found that highly offensive. What you said
was cliché ridden and misinformed. Look, you're entitled to
your views. . .

MEG: It doesn't sound like it.

DICK: Well, I'm entitled to disagree with you, all right. But the
issue for me is why you, as an expatriate, feel compelled to
dump on this place. Because in effect you're dumping on the
people who are actually trying to do things.

MEG: So one can only be critical from the inside. Is that it? Or
perhaps one can't be critical at all?

DICK: You're missing the point.

MEG: The point is, I think that this so called cultural renaissance
is actually about patriotism. Which makes people like you
very defensive.

DICK: That's bullshit.

[*The following dialogue occurs simultaneously.*]

PIP: I think you're the defensive one in this instance.   I didn't
read *The Guardian*. . .

EDWIN: It wasn't worth reading, I think that's the point.

DICK: It was a highly contentious set of opinions.

EDWIN: Which actually misrepresented everything that Meg was on about.

DICK: So you're going to retract that now, are you? That's not what you meant at all. It was the media's fault.

MEG: No, I'm not retracting anything. I stand by what I said.

HIL: What did you say?

MEG: I said that Australians are terrified of any expression of passion. Unless of course the passion is about hedonism and making money. Oh, and sport. Then that's all right. The cultural heroes, the real cultural heroes are good blokes who make a lot o' dough, don't take themselves too seriously and have no pretensions whatsoever about their intellect. You see, you all think I'm terribly pretentious because I take myself seriously. Because I referred to myself as an 'artist'. You think that's pompous bullshit don't you?

MARGE: No. I don't.

DICK: I do.

MEG: [*turning to her sisters*] And you do too, don't you?

PIP: Yeah, I do. 'Cause you're trying to lay a claim that what you do is more important than anyone else.

MEG: I'm doing no such thing Pip.

DICK: You are. Your mythologising the role of the artist. And that is precisely what the cultural movement of this past decade has been about. *De*mythologising it. Cutting away all the rarefied, ivory tower thinking. Making 'culture' accessible to ordinary people.

MEG: And you're suggesting that I'm not. You don't think *Melancholy* is accessible – to 'ordinary' people?

MARGE: Oh yes, of course it is. Absolutely accessible. . .

PIP: It's just your attitude Meg.

MEG: Oh, now I have an attitude problem do I?

[*Pause*]

Well let's talk about attitude shall we? What about when someone writes a novel and gets no response from the people she knows. What can we understand from that? That the novel itself is no good? That novels per se, are not really all that relevant? Or is it something to do with the *attitude* of the other people? Something to do with selfishness? Or what about cowardice ?

PIP: Cowardice? Jesus Christ, Meg. What about the cowardice of someone who can't talk about stuff openly so they have to go and put it in a book.

MEG: Pippa. I can't believe I'm hearing this. From you.

HILARY: What do you want us to say Meg? You've spent the whole time telling us that you don't write autobiography. You write fiction. Now I've had to sit here and listen to all that when you know as well as I do that the only difference is, you haven't used our real names.

SCENE TWELVE

MEG *sits alone on the verandah in half light.* TROY *approaches*

MEG: Troy? What are you doing up?

TROY: I couldn't sleep.

MEG: It's cold. You should go in.

TROY: Meg. [*Pause*] What happened the night my father died?

MEG: I can't tell you.

TROY: Why not?

MEG: Because I promised. [*Bitterly*] It's called loyalty. Keeping a promise even when you know it's wrong.

TROY: Who did you promise?

MEG: Your father.
    [*Silence*]

TROY: Were you having an affair with him?
    [MEG *shakes her head.*]

MEG: Tell me something Troy. Just tell me this first. When Pop said to you that he didn't think I understood about loyalty . . .?

TROY: Yeah.

MEG: Do you think he meant it as a writer or as a person?

[*Pause*]

TROY: I don't know.

[*Pause*]

MEG: The problem with loyalty is that you can keep on and on, living a lie. And you don't even know you're doing it.

[TROY *doesn't understand.*]

I don't know whether you'll be able to make sense of any of this. But I'll tell you anyway. It's not fair otherwise.

[*Pause*]

For quite a long time, I was very much in love with him. Your Dad. I never admitted it. In fact I only admitted it to myself when I was half way through my book. He was such a wonderful man. He was loving and warm and generous. And so funny. He used to make us laugh. Hil and me. We'd be on the floor, holding our stomachs. Absolutely weak with laughter.

[*She smiles at the memory.*]

He was also very sensual. Very affectionate. For those last two years before he died, I thought that he wanted to have an affair with me. I'd got it into my head that he was quite infatuated. And maybe he was. A little bit. But I was resolved that nothing could happen. He was married to my sister. You don't do that. Still, I think if I'm honest. . . I did want something to happen. Anyway that night, I was staying with Dad. The phone rang about midnight and it was Gary. He said he had to meet with me urgently. Somewhere private. So I agreed to meet him on the pier. I got there first and I waited and after a while he came walking up the pier huddled in his jacket. It was very cold and he stood there trying to roll a cigarette and his hands were shaking. He was really agitated. He said, 'Meg, I've done something really stupid'. He was finding it impossible to get the words out. And then he said it, 'I'm having an affair with Pippa'.

[*Long pause.* MEG *daren't look at his face.*]

I'm sorry Troy. I'm sorry it's so shoddy.

TROY: Pippa?

    [MEG *nods. Silence*]

    What did you say?

MEG: I asked him whether Hil knew and he said he didn't think so. . . and then he asked me what he should do. And I said 'End it obviously', and I turned my back and walked down the pier and I never saw him again. I just turned my back. And that was the night he drove his car into a tree. A month later I went to England. . .

    [*Long silence*]

TROY: Do you think he did it on purpose?

MEG: No. You must never think that. It was an accident.

TROY: Does Mum know?

MEG: I don't know what she knows, Troy. She thinks it was me I think.

TROY: That's what everybody thinks.

MEG: I know.

    [TROY *puts his head on* MEG's *shoulder. She puts her arm around him.*]

    I'm sorry Troy.

SCENE THIRTEEN

HILARY *is alone in the garden.* DICK *comes by.*

DICK: Anyone home?

HIL: Hello.

DICK: I just wanted to drop by and thank you for lunch yesterday.

HIL: I'm sorry that it got so tense. It wasn't much fun.

DICK: I.. er. . . wanted to apologise actually. I think I opened a can of worms and. . . well, I didn't let up. It was very. . . insensitive and. . . I'm sorry.

    [*Pause*]

HIL: You weren't to know.

DICK: Well, I think I behaved pretty boorishly. Which no doubt confirms Meg's picture of Australian men.

HIL: I think she was acting pretty boorishly herself.

[*Pause*]

Lethal combination really. Expatriates and Australian men.

[*She looks up and grins.*]

DICK: Marge isn't speaking to me.

[*He grins sheepishly.* HILARY *laughs.*]

HIL: Want a cup of tea?

DICK: No, I'm right thanks.

HIL: She's gone for a walk. Don't worry. You're safe.

[DICK *laughs.*]

DICK: I sat up last night and re-read *Melancholy*.

HIL: Oh, no. Please.

DICK: This is the last time I'll mention it, OK? I promise.

HIL: Good.

DICK: You really are an extraordinary family you know?

HIL: Is that the word for it.

DICK: Browning said this thing, 'When I die, the word 'Italy' will be engraved on my heart.' I couldn't get that out of my mind last night. I kept thinking, 'When I die, what the hell'll be engraved on my heart? Glen Waverley? All the miserable dumps I've lived in?'

[HIL *is looking at him not understanding.*]

See, I realised last night that Meg actually does know what she's got here. . .

HIL: You mean Sorrento?

DICK: No. Not even Sorrento. I mean this house. This family. I feel quite envious of you all. Stupid as it may sound. But I do.

HIL: You're a funny fish.

DICK: Yeah. That's what Marge always says.

SCENE FOURTEEN

MARGE *has set her easel up on the pier facing diagonally across to the beach.* MEG *stands behind appraising the painting. There is a slight awkwardness about them after the events of the preceding evening.*

MEG: I didn't know you were a painter.
MARGE: A weekend painter, I'm afraid.
    [MEG *looks carefully at the painting.*]
MEG: Oh, it's lovely. It's very lovely actually.
    [MARGE *blushes slightly. Silence*]
    Full of yearning.
    [*Silence*]
MARGE: 'Yearning for something that she could not name'
    [MEG *smiles at the reference to her book.*]
    My relationship to this place has changed so much since reading *Melancholy.*
    [*Pause*]
    I didn't get the chance to talk about it with you yesterday, but what I wanted to say was that reading *Melancholy* was just like the experience I had when I first read Helen Garner. I remember reading *Monkey Grip* and thinking, 'This is the place where I live and I've never seen it like this before'. It was as though she'd given me the summer in the inner suburbs. Like it hadn't existed until I read her book. And all of a sudden, everything became meaningful - going down to the Fitzroy pool - Aqua Profunda – and walking to the shop on one of those hot evenings and smelling the asphalt. Watching those young women in their cotton dresses riding their bicycles through the park. She gave it to me. She gave it life.
MEG: Mmm. I know exactly what you mean.
MARGE: I feel the same about Sorrento. It's not just the pretty little place that I come to every weekend for a bit of R & R. Not any more. I've started to feel that I *need* to come here. I take that walk often you know - from the back beach across

the headlands towards Portsea. And I think I've found the place Grace calls 'The Great Rock'. '. . .perched on the fartherest point, with the steepest fall, a place for glorious departure.'

[MEG *smiles.*]

It's so wild, with the wind and the surf smashing around over the rocks. Way down there at the foot of the cliffs. I feel as though you've awakened something in me. It's like a yearning, a real yearning . . .to. . . feel again.

[*Pause*]

One closes down on one's passions so much. I suppose I always used to choose the sheltered spots. . . [like Helen] but now. . . I feel this urgency. . . to be part of it all, part of the expanse.

[MEG *is deeply touched by* MARGE's *outburst.*]

I always used to paint with watercolour you know, but now I've started to use oils.

SCENE FIFTEEN

PIPPA *is wandering restlessly around the living room.* EDWIN *enters.*

EDWIN: I was looking for Meg.

PIP: So was I.

EDWIN: Oh, by the way, I finished that book you lent me.

PIPPA: Uh huh.

[MEG *enters, unseen by* EDWIN.]

EDWIN: Yes, I realised that I have a bit of a problem with Australian novels. They're so hampered by an obsession with the vernacular. It utterly constrains them. I don't know. The Australian language – it's really a language for such tawdry dreams. [EDWIN *realises* MEG *has been present.*] Oh. I was just off to bed.

MEG: OK.

EDWIN: Will you be long?

MEG: I don't know.

EDWIN: Mmm. All right. I'll see you later. I haven't seen that much of you lately. I thought perhaps we could go for a little walk. Before bed. But perhaps tomorrow.

MEG: Yeah.

[*Pause*]

PIPPA: Good night Edwin.

EDWIN: Oh. All right.

[EDWIN *leaves.*]

PIPPA: I think we need to talk about a few things.

MEG: Yes. We do.

[MEG *looks at the painting. She moves over to it and straightens it up.*]

PIP: What are you doing?

MEG: Oh, just looking at this. [*She smiles.*] It's a bloody awful painting isn't it? We really should take it down. . .

PIP: No. Leave it. . . Sorry. Please leave it.

[*She takes a deep breath and talks in a measured way.*]
I know you think that this house means nothing to me. You think I don't feel things as strongly as you do. . .

MEG: That's not true.

PIP: I don't think that you believe I feel any real sentiment about this house. But you're wrong. I do. Regardless of what I feel, I think we should encourage Hil to move out.

[*Pause*]
This place is dying, Meg. The heart and soul of this house, this town, disappeared with Dad. Vanished - presumed dead. But it's not dead yet. It's just dying. Don't you feel it? We're living with the dying because there's no body. No burial. And there will never be a burial until we sell this house. For Hilary's sake. . . I'm really begging you. . . Meg. . . she will shrivel up here - like Mum, and it's not right. She has to salvage her life. . .

[*She starts to cry, heavy sobs.* MEG *puts her arms around her.*]

MEG: Oh, Pippy. Pippy Long Stocking.

[MEG *hugs her, stroking her hair until* PIP *pulls away.*]

PIP: Please? Meg? Will you talk to her?

[MEG *stares at the floor. Her heart is in turmoil.*]

MEG: I'll only talk to her. . . if you will.

[*Silence*]

PIP: She doesn't want to know, Meg. Believe me. She doesn't want to know.

MEG: I want her to know.

PIP: It just makes things worse, Meg. Don't you see. And it's not going to bring him back.

SCENE SIXTEEN

In the pitch black there is a scream. HILARY *sits on the edge of* TROY*'s bed. He has woken in a sweat after a nightmare. She tries to console him.*

TROY: I got cold Mum. I had to come in.

HIL: I know. Ssh.

TROY: I went to get my towel. And when I turned back. . .

HIL: Ssh.

TROY: He was gone.

HIL: I know darling.

TROY: I just turned my back. I turned my back. And now. . . every night. . .

HIL: Oh, my darling boy. . . my dear, darling boy.

TROY: And it's the same one. I'm talking to someone. And I turn my back and when I look around. . . they're gone. They disappear. Oh, Mum. Mum. I can't stand it.

HIL: They'll stop. They will. I promise you.

TROY: Every night. . . I'm standing on the sand, Mum. And I look out to sea and I search and search the waves and I try and see him. And I think I see him.

[*He starts to sob.*]

But I didn't do anything. I just ran away.

[HILARY *takes him firmly by the shoulders.*]

HILARY: Troy, listen to me. You didn't see anything. By the time you looked back there was nothing there. If there was something, Troy. . . if he'd been calling you, or waving his arms. . .if you'd seen anything, you would have gone back in there. I know you would. And not because you're brave - even though you are - you're the bravest kid I know. But you would have done it, Troy. Just on instinct. I know that more than I know anything in the whole world. But you didn't, you see, because there was nothing there. There was only the sea.

[*Pause*]

One day, Troyby, one day. . . we'll walk along the back beach and we'll look out at the sea and we won't be frightened by it any more. We'll say, 'This is what happened'.

[*Pause*]

We don't know why, but what we do know is that it didn't happen to you and it didn't happen to me. We're the lucky ones.

[*Pause*]

We've got a lot to feel sorry for - you and me. God knows. But I'm buggered if I'm gonna go under. And I'm not gonna let you either.

SCENE SEVENTEEN

EDWIN *stands looking out to sea on the jetty as* MARGE *paints.* MEG *wanders up the jetty toward them.*

EDWIN: [*to* MARGE] Sometimes I have this very strange feeling of having been here before. It all seems so familiar. Then at other times it's not at all like what I imagined. It's very odd.

MARGE: How is it different to what you imagined?

EDWIN: It isn't as harsh. The light. In fact it's very gentle. . . very mellow.

MARGE: Rather melancholy?

EDWIN: Yes. [*He smiles.*] I suppose that's why I feel I know the place. Odd isn't it?

MARGE: No, not at all. It's a very powerful evocation of the place.

EDWIN: Yes, it is isn't it? I hadn't really appreciated that before I came. She writes with such a potent sense of place and I haven't really understood before just how central it is to her writing.

MARGE: It's the life source of the novel I would have thought.

EDWIN: Yes.

    [*Pause*]

I wonder whether it's the life source for the novelist.

    [MARGE *nods thoughtfully. There is a pensive silence.*]

You know. . . the great irony is that she's being accused here of 'borrowing' from real life, at least that's what her sisters are suggesting, and yet in London there are certain critics who've argued that it's derivative of other fiction.

    [MEG *wanders up.*]

MARGE: British critics?

    [EDWIN *nods.*]

That'd be right. They can't conceive that anything original could be produced here; that something of beauty, profundity or passion could arise from an experience that's essentially Australian.

EDWIN: I don't think it's a question of a lack of originality.

MEG: No, it's only a question of quality isn't it? Being written in a language of such tawdry dreams?

    [*Silence*]

MARGE: You could hardly put *Melancholy* in that category.

MEG: Oh, perhaps you could. Perhaps it's all about tawdry little dreams.

EDWIN: Oh, come on Meg.

    [*Silence*]

MARGE: Edwin, could you imagine yourself living here?

    [EDWIN *is non-commital. Silence.* MEG *looks at him wanting him to take the question seriously.*]

MEG: Could you?

EDWIN: Here? In Sorrento? I don't think so.

MARGE: What about Australia?

    [*Long pause*]

MEG: Could you? You haven't answered the question.

MARGE: And you Meg? Have you?

SCENE EIGHTEEN

HILARY *sits by the window of the sitting room.* PIP *enters. She gives* HILARY *a small pile of clothes.*

PIP: Here, you can have these if you want. I can't fit them in.

    [*Pause*]

I don't care what you decide about the house now. It's up to you. It doesn't affect me. It's really about you and Troy. What you want to do in the future. But I want to take this. [*The painting*] That's all I want. You can have everything else. And I want to take it with me now, because I might never come back.

    [*She attempts to unhook the painting.*]

HILARY: Leave it! None of us might ever come back. But until we decide, that stays where it is.

PIPPA: You successfully manage every time to divest me of any sense of belonging, don't you? You won't say it, you won't admit it but you really believe that this house and this family is yours. . .

HILARY: What family? What family are you talking about? There is no family any more.

PIP: No. Because you won't share it. You want to own it!

HILARY: I've never owned anything in my whole life. Damn you! I never even owned my own marriage. Damn you. Damn you. . .

    [MEG *stands at the door.*]

And damn you!

    [MEG *is silent.*]

MEG: It's about time you started. It's about time we all started. To own what's happened to us.

PIP: Why Meg? So we can all write best sellers?

MEG: Yes. All right, let's talk about best sellers. I wrote that book. And I didn't steal anything from you or you or anyone else who wants to lay claims to ownership.

HIL: But you don't Meg. You don't own what's happened. Don't you see that?

MEG: No. I only own my story. And that's a very small thing.

PIP: Oh, yes it's your book. Your story all right. It's got your name written all over it. But it's our integrity. That's what you've stolen.

[*Silence*]

MEG: Is that what you think? Do you really believe that I have robbed you of your integrity? Because if I'm guilty of that, I'll recall every single copy of that book from every publisher and every bookshop in the world. I'll withdraw it from the Booker prize right now. . . if that's what you think.

[*Pause*]

But I always thought that integrity was something that couldn't be given or taken away. That it was the only thing a person could own.

[*Silence*]

D'you know why I came home? Because I wanted to see if I could fit into this family again. I wanted to see if the three of us could be together. I want to know now, whether you two think it's possible?

[*Silence*]

You'll never forgive me, will you, for writing about something that we couldn't talk about.

HIL: Did we ever try? Did we ever really try?

[*The three women maintain their position in a freeze. Music plays.*]

SCENE NINETEEN

Music continues as the three women maintain their freeze.

AUCTIONEER: [*voice over*] Ladies and gentlemen. I'd like to take this opportunity to welcome you all to the auction of number one Ti-Tree Road, Sorrento. It's not often that a property in such a glorious location as this, comes on to the market and we're very pleased indeed to be offering it to you today. We've sold many, many properties on the peninsular and I can assure you that prices are escalating every week. Investment opportunities like this one don't come your way very often. This is a holiday makers paradise. And with this beautiful location the possibilities are endless: holiday flats, guest houses, even a luxury hotel. What a beautiful site for a hotel. Ladies and gentlemen, I offer you number one Ti-tree Road Sorrento. Who'd like to give me a reasonable offer?

THE END

From Stage to Screen

Peter Fitzpatrick and Richard Franklin

In a number of ways *Hotel Sorrento* was a 'natural' subject for screen adaptation. The episodic structure which seems to pre-empt a thoroughly naturalistic treatment on stage, at least in terms of the play's design, lends itself well to cinematic cross cutting. The characters were engaging and well differentiated, and the attractions of the coast and town of Sorrento as a 'real' location – the spaciousness and natural beauty which no theatre could do more than imply – offered wonderful possibilities for the camera and obviated the traditional somewhat erroneous notion of having to 'open out' theatre on film.

Moreover, two or three years after the play's first appearance, the spirit of millennial republicanism had added a new urgency to the cultural debate. The subject of Australia's independence, as an issue that mattered emotionally and imaginatively as well as politically and historically, was suddenly very much on the agenda again. This time for an audience that was potentially much wider than the one which had responded so positively to *Hotel Sorrento* on stage.

The success of the film since its release in April 1995 testifies to those intrinsic qualities and, perhaps, to the timeliness of the project. Inevitably, though, the process of translation from stage to screen involved losses as well as gains. It is almost axiomatic that, since a picture is understood to be worth a thousand words, one of the first sacrifices is dialogue. Even an adaptation that set out, as this one did, to retain most of the intelligent conversation that Hannie Rayson wrote, was not exempt from the need to shift the delicate balance slightly from verbal to visual. While we tried hard to retain most of the sisters' speeches (indeed Pippa gained some cinematic weighting) Dick lost his bohemian past and Marge never made it to the 'great rock'.

It is not, of course, a simple case of serious talk being in itself less appropriate to the screen and we were eager to prove that long dialogue scenes can work just as well. *Hotel Sorrento* the film, holds seven characters around a lunch table for an uninterrupted 11 minutes, maintaining the sense of group presence by frequent cross-cutting and occasional group shots, but also focusing points of tension by shuffling through a number of pairings. Where so many personal and cultural conflicts rise to the surface, there are positive advantages in the limiting frame afforded by the screen. The full awareness of the group as a composite is, most of the time, only available to the cinema viewer by inference. The capacity to direct attention not merely to the speaker but to the most significant listener(s) gives great power to the camera, particularly during the eloquent silences between speeches. Shifting attention for instance from the initial points of natural conflict between established 'couples' like Meg and Edwin, and Dick and Marge through the initial pairing in a two shot of the 'writers' Dick and Meg, then moving rapidly as they do, into opposition and their own separate shots. The dialogue here mostly survives, and may even gain something from the intensity of the close-up which the theatre cannot provide.

The film also extends the cultural debate a little, by allowing Pippa to articulate a form of imperialism which is more conspicuous and immediate to contemporary Australian audiences and these discussions are supported visually by all the little bits of American iconography glimpsed in the Sorrento streets. American audiences have been appalled that their worst films and fast food have made it to provincial Victoria.

In the end, the principal loss on film is in what is asked of the collaborative imagination of the viewer. It is the 'down-side' of cinema's capacity to make the experience seem more real, to actually do the thing-in-itself that in the theatre always involves a willing suspension of disbelief. Film can present the actual main street of Sorrento, just a little modified for the purpose, and can capture the play of light on the water as it laps around the jetty. It can take the viewer into the kitchen or back yard, and can even provide a facsimile of a London mews, actually shot in Melbourne. What it weakens is the symbolic relationship between all these places that is fundamental to the composite and metaphorical set for any production of Hannie Rayson's play, as it is to its script. So the nexus between sea and shore, between the house and the horizon, loses some of its force, and in a narrative in which Australia is dramatised not only as a colonial culture turning inward in a cringe, but more positively as a coastal culture always looking out, that is a significant cost. In the theatre that improbable linkage of locations is a constant sign of the emotional ties which hold these sisters together.

Rayson's play invites the process of 'realisation', in the literal sense, and gains a good deal from it. Its quality stands up to the scrutiny invited by a medium in which the flicker of any eyelid can fill a giant screen. But its power as a piece of theatre will also survive translation into a form which makes many of its images seem real and permanent. The great thing about film is its permanence, but it is also its failing. There are unlikely to be any more versions of *Hotel Sorrento* the film, but *Hotel Sorrento* the play is likely to be re-made many times as part of a national repertoire.

July 1995